It's All About the Elizabeths:

A Financial Management Guide for Canadian Teens

Suzanne Kleinberg

Other Books by Suzanne Kleinberg

From Playstation® to Workstation: A Career Guide for Generation Text Surviving in a Baby Boomer World.

Employee Rights and Employer Wrongs: A Laymen's Guide to Your Rights in the Workplace

It's All About the Elizabeths:

A Financial Management Guide for Canadian Teens

Suzanne Kleinberg

Potential To Soar Publishing
Toronto, Canada

Cover images used and altered with the permission of the Bank of Canada.

Canadian Cataloguing in Publication Data

Library and Archives Canada Cataloguing in Publication

Kleinberg, Suzanne, 1963-
      It's all about the Elizabeths : a financial management guide for Canadian teens / Suzanne Kleinberg ; Michael Kreimeh, illustrator. – 1st ed.

Includes index.
ISBN 978-0-9866684-1-8

      1. Teenagers--Finance, Personal. 2. Finance, Personal.
I. Kreimeh, Michael, 1970-   II. Title.

HG179.K6 2010   332.02400835   C2010-905215-3

Potential To Soar Publishing
Thornhill, Ontario

Dedication

To my mother, Frances, a woman before her time, who instilled in me early on that success and independence cannot come without financial responsibility.

Table of Contents

Introduction

"If you think nobody cares if you are alive,
try missing a couple of car payments."
-- Anonymous

Remember when your only financial concern was making your allowance last the whole week? Well, those days are over! As you approach adulthood, you are responsible for managing your own finances. As overwhelming as this may be, the sooner you get a handle on your financial situation and your options, the more skilled you will be at avoiding common pitfalls that could have you enslaved in debt for years. If you get control of your finances and understand them now, then you will have a lot less stress later on.

Some people hate planning but it is vital that you prepare yourself financially. As we age, expenses tend to increase...from kids who want toys; to teens who want expensive clothes and iPhones; to adults buying a home, a car, getting married....and so on. Unexpected things happen all the time - so being financially ready for it makes life much easier. People who don't financially plan will often find themselves living from paycheque to paycheque or struggling to come up with money when something occurs unexpectedly. Not to worry though, usually those who don't have financial plans in place can easily create one to get themselves out of debt.

Sounds easy? Well, clearly it is not when you look at some of the statistics on debt for young adults. (Source: Charles Schwab US 2007)

- On average, 30% of the monthly income of young adults between 18-24 years old goes to debt repayment (i.e. credit card interest, car or student loan interest, etc.).
- 29% of teens are in debt.
- 45% of teens know how to use a credit card yet only 26% understand credit card interest charges and fees.
- Only 33% of teens know how to read a bank statement, balance a chequebook and pay bills.
- Only 20% of teens know how to invest money.
- The number of people between 18-24 years old who have declared bankruptcy in 2007 has increased 96% in ten years.

In this book, we will review a lot of the realities about income and expenses as well as savings and investments. At the end, you will have the opportunity to put together a budget to understand your current financial snapshot.

Preface

Money, money, money! It appears that a lot of us in today's society can never get enough. However, in most cases, the problem is not that we don't have enough; it is that we don't know how to effectively manage it. As a result, Canadians are experiencing record levels of debt. High levels of debt affect us all.

This is why it is essential that teens learn the importance of financial planning long before they are out on their own. Without this knowledge, mistakes could lead them into serious money troubles including credit problems, collection agency harassment, identity theft and/or bankruptcy.

To avoid today's problems, teens need to know more than just putting money into a savings account for a rainy day. They need to understand all the options and the pitfalls out there. They need to understand not only the importance of a budget but how to effectively complete one. They need to have a clear vision of what it costs to live on your own in a Canadian city. They also definitely need to know about taxes and how much of their income it can eat away.

Currently, there are few publications available specifically for teens in the marketplace. Through practical examples and exercises, teens can easily gain confidence in the key basics of money management. This book was written to address the gap in the accessibility of this information and to provide useful exercises so that the upcoming generation does not repeat the missteps of the current generation.

Gross Income
TAXES & DEDUCTIONS
Canada Pension Plan
Employment Insurance
Benefits
RRSP's
Net Income

What You Earn Is Not What You Get

Salary and Taxes

It is always exciting to get a new job that pays more than the last one. However, the joy seems to fade when we get our first pay cheque and see all the taxes and the costs of company benefits taken off. *Before* you get any pay cheque, whether it is an actual cheque or deposited in your bank account by your employer (known as "direct deposit"), it is required by law that your employer withdraw taxes owed prior to paying you. So don't be shocked if you start your first job expecting a big cheque after your first two weeks on the job and see something totally different in your bank account.

Because of the Canadian tax code, the more you earn, the higher your tax rate. In the table below, you will see that the higher salary pays a higher tax rate. There is no difference in tax rates if you are a salaried employee (i.e. full time with a determined yearly salary) vs. a part time employee who gets an hourly wage. The tax rate is based on the expected total income for the full calendar year. Here are examples for each province:

2011 Alberta

	Example A	Example B	Example C
Annual Income	$26,000.00	$52,000.00	$100,000.00
Gross **weekly** pay	**$500.00**	**$1,000.00**	**$1,923.08**
Federal Tax	$75.00	$164.07	$380.16
Provincial Tax	$50.00	$100.00	$192.31
CPP (4.95% up to $2,217.60)	$21.42	$46.17	$91.86
EI (1.78% up to $780.36)	$8.90	$17.80	$34.23
Net Amount*	**$344.68**	**$671.96**	**$1,224.52**

2011 British Columbia

	Example A	Example B	Example C
Annual Income	$26,000.00	$52,000.00	$100,000.00
Gross **weekly** pay	**$500.00**	**$1,000.00**	**$1,923.08**
Federal Tax	$75.00	$164.07	$380.16
Provincial Tax	$25.30	$58.65	$150.50
CPP (4.95% up to $2,217.60)	$21.42	$46.17	$91.86
EI (1.78% up to $780.36)	$8.90	$17.80	$34.23
Net Amount*	**$369.38**	**$713.31**	**$1,266.33**

2011 Manitoba

	Example A	Example B	Example C
Annual Income	$26,000.00	$52,000.00	$100,000.00
Gross **weekly** pay	**$500.00**	**$1,000.00**	**$1,923.08**
Federal Tax	$75.00	$164.07	$380.16
Provincial Tax	$54.00	$115.88	$263.08
CPP (4.95% up to $2,217.60)	$21.42	$46.17	$91.86
EI (1.73% up to $780.36)	$8.90	$17.80	$34.23
Net Amount*	**$340.68**	**$656.08**	**$1,153.75**

2011 New Brunswick

	Example A	Example B	Example C
Annual Income	$26,000.00	$52,000.00	$100,000.00
Gross **weekly** pay	**$500.00**	**$1,000.00**	**$1,923.08**
Federal Tax	$75.00	$164.07	$380.16
Provincial Tax	$45.50	$99.57	$212.78
CPP (4.95% up to $2,217.60)	$21.42	$46.17	$91.86
EI (1.73% up to $780.36)	$8.90	$17.80	$34.23
Net Amount*	**$349.18**	**$672.39**	**$1,204.05**

2011 Newfoundland & Labrador

	Example A	Example B	Example C
Annual Income	$26,000.00	$52,000.00	$100,000.00
Gross **weekly** pay	**$500.00**	**$1,000.00**	**$1,923.08**
Federal Tax	$75.00	$164.07	$380.16
Provincial Tax	$38.50	$95.55	$216.50
CPP (4.95% up to $2,217.60)	$21.42	$46.17	$91.86
EI (1.73% up to $780.36)	$8.90	$17.80	$34.23
*Net Amount**	**$356.18**	**$676.41**	**$1,200.33**

2011 Northwest Territories

	Example A	Example B	Example C
Annual Income	$26,000.00	$52,000.00	$100,000.00
Gross **weekly** pay	**$500.00**	**$1,000.00**	**$1,923.08**
Federal Tax	$75.00	$164.07	$380.16
Provincial Tax	$29.50	$66.46	$162.98
CPP (4.95% up to $2,217.60)	$21.42	$46.17	$91.86
EI (1.73% up to $780.36)	$8.90	$17.80	$34.23
*Net Amount**	**$365.18**	**$705.50**	**$1,253.85**

2011 Nova Scotia

	Example A	Example B	Example C
Annual Income	$26,000.00	$52,000.00	$100,000.00
Gross **weekly** pay	**$500.00**	**$1,000.00**	**$1,923.08**
Federal Tax	$75.00	$164.07	$380.16
Provincial Tax	$43.95	$114.45	$267.07
CPP (4.95% up to $2,217.60)	$21.42	$46.17	$91.86
EI (1.73% up to $780.36)	$8.90	$17.80	$34.23
*Net Amount**	**$350.73**	**$657.51**	**$1,149.76**

2011 Nunavut

	Example A	Example B	Example C
Annual Income	$26,000.00	$52,000.00	$100,000.00
Gross **weekly** pay	**$500.00**	**$1,000.00**	**$1,923.08**
Federal Tax	$75.00	$164.07	$380.16
Provincial Tax	$20.00	$47.15	$119.75
CPP (4.95% up to $2,217.60)	$21.42	$46.17	$91.86
EI (1.73% up to $780.36)	$8.90	$17.80	$34.23
*Net Amount**	**$374.68**	**$724.81**	**$1,297.08**

2011 Ontario

	Example A	Example B	Example C
Annual Income	$26,000.00	$52,000.00	$100,000.00
Gross **weekly** pay	**$500.00**	**$1,000.00**	**$1,923.08**
Federal Tax	$75.00	$164.07	$380.16
Provincial Tax	$25.25	$61.72	$155.63
CPP (4.95% up to $2,217.60)	$21.42	$46.17	$91.86
EI (1.73% up to $780.36)	$8.90	$17.80	$34.23
Net Amount*	**$369.43**	**$710.24**	**$1,261.20**

2011 Prince Edward Island

	Example A	Example B	Example C
Annual Income	$26,000.00	$52,000.00	$100,000.00
Gross **weekly** pay	**$500.00**	**$1,000.00**	**$1,923.08**
Federal Tax	$75.00	$164.07	$380.16
Provincial Tax	$49.00	$113.40	$260.88
CPP (4.95% up to $2,217.60)	$21.42	$46.17	$91.86
EI (1.73% up to $780.36)	$8.90	$17.80	$34.23
Net Amount*	**$345.68**	**$658.56**	**$1,155.95**

2011 Québec

	Example A	Example B	Example C
Annual Income	$26,000.00	$52,000.00	$100,000.00
Gross **weekly** pay	**$500.00**	**$1,000.00**	**$1,923.08**
Federal Tax	$75.00	$164.07	$380.16
Provincial Tax	$80.00	$169.95	$371.40
CPP (4.95% up to $2,217.60)	$21.42	$46.17	$91.86
EI (1.41% up to $786.76)	$7.05	$14.10	$27.12
Net Amount*	**$316.53**	**$605.71**	**$1,052.54**

2011 Saskatchewan

	Example A	Example B	Example C
Annual Income	$26,000.00	$52,000.00	$100,000.00
Gross **weekly** pay	**$500.00**	**$1,000.00**	**$1,923.08**
Federal Tax	$75.00	$164.07	$380.16
Provincial Tax	$55.00	$114.26	$234.26
CPP (4.95% up to $2,217.60)	$21.42	$46.17	$91.86
EI (1.73% up to $780.36)	$8.90	$17.80	$34.23
Net Amount*	**$339.68**	**$657.70**	**$1,182.57**

2011 Yukon

	Example A	Example B	Example C
Annual Income	$26,000.00	$52,000.00	$100,000.00
Gross **weekly** pay	**$500.00**	**$1,000.00**	**$1,923.08**
Federal Tax	$75.00	$164.07	$380.16
Provincial Tax	$35.20	$75.70	$170.78
CPP (4.95% up to $2,217.60)	$21.42	$46.17	$91.86
EI (1.73% up to $780.36)	$8.90	$17.80	$34.23
*Net Amount**	**$359.48**	**$696.26**	**$1,246.05**

*Does *not* include costs of company pensions, benefits, or insurance that is withdrawn from your pay.

CPP (Canadian Pension Plan) is money from the government that you will receive monthly after age 65 similar to a salary. The amount you receive depends on the amount that you have paid into the system throughout the years. When calculating, there is a $3500 annual exemption. For more information: http://www.servicecanada.gc.ca/eng/sc/cpp/retirement/canadapension.shtml

EI (Employment Insurance) is the bi-weekly money that you receive when you are unemployed. Check with the Federal government website on how to qualify. For more information: http://www.servicecanada.gc.ca/eng/sc/ei/benefits/regular.shtml. Even if you have never received Employment Insurance benefits or never intend to, you must still pay this tax.

Don't assume that these taxes are the total amount of tax that you will be accountable for. If your employer underestimates your annual earnings (e.g. if you get a bonus or a raise during the year), then you may be required to pay more taxes when you complete your tax return next April. Keep that in mind when you are spending your earnings!

Important rates to be aware of:

2011 Federal Income Tax

Net Income	Tax
$0 to $41,544	15%
Between $41,545 and $83,088	22%
Between $83,089 and $128,800	26%
Over $128,800	29%
Source: Canada Revenue Agency - 2011.	

2011 Provincial Income Tax

Provincial / Territorial tax rates	
Provinces / Territories	Rate(s)
Newfoundland and Labrador	7.7% on the first $31,904 of taxable income + 12.5% on the next $31,903 + 13.3% on the amount over $63,807
Prince Edward Island	9.8% on the first $31,984 of taxable income + 13.8% on the next $31,985 + 16.7% on the amount over $63,969
Nova Scotia	8.79% on the first $29,590 of taxable income + 14.95% on the next $29,590 + 16.67% on the next $33,820 + 17.5% on the next $57,000 21% on the amount over $150,000
New Brunswick	9.1% on the first $37,149 of taxable income + 12.1% on the next $36,422 + 12.4% on the next $46,496 + 12.7% on the amount over $120,796
Québec	16% on the first $39,060 + 20% on the next $39,060 + 24% on the amount over $78,120

Ontario	5.05% on the first $37,774 of taxable income + 9.15% on the next $37,776 + 11.16% on the amount over $75,550
Manitoba	10.8% on the first $31,000 of taxable income + 12.75% on the next $36,000 + 17.4% on the amount over $67,000
Saskatchewan	11% on the first $40,919 of taxable income + 13% on the next $75,992 + 15% on the amount over $116,911
Alberta	10% of taxable income
British Columbia	5.06% on the first $36,146 of taxable income + 7.7% on the next $36,147 + 10.5% on the next $10,708 + 12.29% on the next $17,786 + 14.7% on the amount over $100,787
Yukon	7.04% on the first $41,544 of taxable income + 9.68% on the next $41,544 + 11.44% on the next $45,712 + 12.76% on the amount over $128,800
Northwest Territories	5.9% on the first $37,626 of taxable income + 8.6% on the next $37,627 + 12.2% on the next $47,092 + 14.05% on the amount over $122,345
Nunavut	4% on the first $39,612 of taxable income + 7% on the next $39,612 + 9% on the next $49,576 + 11.5% on the amount over $128,800

How do these rates work?

For example, if you earned $130,000 per year in the Yukon, how much would you owe the federal and provincial governments in income taxes (excluding all deductions and adjustments)?

First, let's calculate the federal amount:

	Up to $41,544 at 15%	Between $41,545 and $83,088 at 22%	Between $83,089 and $128,800 at 26%	Over $128,800 at 29%
Calculation	41544 * 0.15	(83088 - 41544) * 0.22	(128800-83088) * 0.26	(130000 – 128800) * 0.29
Amount	$ 6,231.60 +	$ 9,139.68 +	$ 11,885.12 +	$ 348.00 =
Total Federal Tax	$27,604.40			

Now, let's calculate the provincial amount for the Yukon Territories:

	Up to $41,544 at 7.04%	Between $41,545 and $83,088 at 9.68%	Between $83,089 and $128,800 at 11.44%	Over $128,800 at 12.76%
Calculation	41544 * 0.0704	(83088-41544) * 0.0968	(128800-83088) * 0.1144	(130000 – 128800) * 0.1276
Amount	$ 2,924.70 +	$ 4,021.46 +	$ 5,229.45 +	$ 153.12 =
Total Provincial Tax	$12,328.73			

The total Federal and Provincial (Yukon) income tax for 2010 on $130,000 would be: $27,604.40 + $12,328.73 = **$39,933.13**

That's an average of almost 31% of your salary!!

And that is just the income tax. There are other deductions from your paycheque as well, including Canada Pension Plan, Employment Insurance Premiums, and any taxable benefits you may receive from your employer and so on.

Keep this in mind when you are creating a budget. Your salary and your "take home" pay are two totally different amounts.

✎ Exercise: Calculate the Tax

Now you try the previous example for yourself. Use the following tables to calculate the following federal and provincial income tax amounts:

1) $40,000 salary in PEI

Federal:

	Up to $41,544 at 15%	Between $41,545 and $83,088 at 22%	Between $83.089 and $128,800 at 26%	Over $128,800 at 29%
Calculation				
Amount	$ +	$ +	$ +	$ =
Total Federal Tax	$			

Provincial (PEI):

	Up to $31,984 at 9.8%	Between $31,985 and $63,969 at 13.8%	Over $63,969 at 16.7%
Calculation			
Amount	$ +	$ +	$ +
Total Provincial Tax	$		

2) $102,000 salary in Ontario

Federal:

	Up to $41,544 at 15%	Between $41,545 and $83,088 at 22%	Between $83.089 and $128,800 at 26%	Over $128,800 at 29%
Calculation				
Amount	$ +	$ +	$ +	$ =
Total Federal Tax	$			

Provincial (Ontario):

	Up to $37,774 at 5.05%	Between $37,775 and $75,550 at 9.15%	Over $75,550 at 11.16%
Calculation			
Amount	$ +	$ +	$ =
Total Provincial Tax	$		

Answers: See Appendix D

Current Provincial Minimum Wage

Each province and territory has its own minimum wage. Any increases in the minimum wage are regulated by the province or territory. Therefore, one provincial government's increase to the minimum wage is no guarantee that other provinces will follow accordingly.

Province	Minimum Wage (2011)
Alberta	$8.80
BC	$8.00 $6.00 "First Job" Rate (less than 500 hours of work experience and no paid experience before November 2001)
Saskatchewan	$9.25
Manitoba	$9.50
Ontario	$10.25 General Workers $8.90 Liquor Servers $9.60 Student Under 18 (less than 28 hrs/wk)
Québec	Before May 2011: $9.50 General Workers $8.25 If Gratuities Apply As of May 2011: $9.65 General Workers $8.35 If Gratuities Apply
New Brunswick	$9.00
Nova Scotia	$9.65

PEI	$9.00
Newfoundland & Labrador	$10.00
Yukon	$8.93
NWT	$9.00
Nunavut	$11.00
Federal Rate	Going rate of province in which you work (e.g. if you work full-time for the Federal government and work in Ontario, then the minimum wage would be $10.25.)

Bank On It

Is your piggy-bank getting stuffed with cash? Nice! Now is the time to start thinking about opening a bank account. Let these tips help guide you when determining which type of bank account is right for you.

The Basics:

So why should you keep your money in a bank account? There are many reasons. Security is at the top of the list. Bank accounts hold your money for you and help you increase your savings by paying you interest. A bank account also enables you to pay your bills online, by cheque or at the bank in-person.

It is important to compare the different options available to you. The types of bank accounts include savings, chequing and mixed:

- **Savings accounts**, as you can probably guess, help you save money! You can withdraw money when you want but they are really designed to help you hold on to your money and earn interest on it. Interest rates are usually quite low (usually between 1% and 3% per year).

- **Chequing accounts** are designed for purchasing and payment activities. They usually offer lower interest rates (if any) and higher transaction fees but allow you to write cheques, pay bills online and email money transfers. Most banks will provide various plans that will charge you a single monthly fee for a specified number of transactions (for example, $9.95 per month for 3 cheques plus one email transfer plus 10 ATM or online banking transactions).

- **Mixed accounts** are part savings and part chequing. You can perform chequing account transactions in addition to getting a certain interest rate to still encourage saving.

🖎 Exercise: Chequing Plans: Which would you rather?

Which would you rather?

Review the following banking plans (columns 3 and 4) including the rates for individual transactions if you are not on a plan (column 2). Look at the average monthly usage proposed in the first column. Try to pick the best plan for the cost.

Your average monthly use	Bank Individual Rates	Plan 1	Plan 2
Debit card use (including ATM) averages 15 times/mo. Cheque use 2 times/mo. Email transfers 2 times/mo. Online banking payments 10 times/mo.	Debit card = $0.30 per use Cheques = $0.50 each Email transfers = $1.50 per use Online bank transactions = $0.25 per use	$15.00/mo. Includes: 25 debit card uses 5 cheques 4 email transfers 20 online banking (any uses above the plan allowed will be charged at the bank individual rates)	$7.95/mo. Includes: 30 debit card and/or online banking uses 2 cheques per month 1 email transfer (any uses above the plan allowed will be charged at the bank individual rates)
	Average monthly total cost without a plan is $11.00	While this appears to be a good deal, your usage is not this high so this plan would be too expensive.	True cost: $7.95 plus overages: Email transfer: $1.50 + 5 Debit Card/Online at $1.50 = $10.95

While Plan 1 *appears* to be a good deal, it is not a good deal for you unless you plan on increasing your monthly transactions greatly. You won't be able to experience the savings that are intended for users of this plan. If you minimize your transactions where possible, Plan 2 may be the most economical, especially if you don't exceed the transactions allowed by the plan.

Check out the various plans available at your bank and determine which, if any, would be suitable for you now and which plan would be suitable a few years from now when you are living on your own.

If you already have a bank account, check your past few monthly statements or track your usage to see if your current plan (if any) is the best for you. Check with your bank to see if you can save money on a different plan.

Tips:

- Before you choose a bank account, shop around to see what service fees each institution charges and the rates of interest that they pay. Some banks charge you for withdrawing money with your bank card, writing cheques, paying bills online or getting service in-person from a teller at a bank branch.

- Save time by banking online. Online banking (or e-banking) is one of the most popular banking activities and it's not hard to see why. You can do almost all of your transactions online, from opening a new account and paying bills to investing in a Registered Retirement Savings Plan (RRSP).

- Have money to invest? Talk to a professional financial planner. He or she can work with you to develop an investment plan that can help you save money and get ready for retirement (it may seem a long way away, but the earlier you start, the more money you'll have in the end). A Financial Planner will explain the different types of investments available to you and help you define your financial priorities. He / she can also assist you with investments that will minimize your taxes (see RRSP further in this chapter).

- Do you have valuables that need protection, such as jewellery or legal documents? Most banks offer safe deposit boxes where, for a fee, you can store your valuables in a secure space in which only you and the bank have a key. The fees vary depending on the size of the box you rent. In some cases, this fee may be tax deductible.

Minimum Monthly Balance

Many institutions waive the monthly service fees on certain accounts if you maintain a minimum monthly balance in your account. Depending on the financial institution and the type of account, minimum balances range from $1,000 to $5,000. On most accounts, however, the minimum balance is generally $1,000 or $2,000.

Maintaining a minimum monthly balance can sometimes waive the monthly fee associated with your banking package. However, any cost savings should be compared to the returns or other opportunities you forego by keeping your money in your bank account (this concept is known as "opportunity cost"). For example, if you have a loan, it may be more cost-effective to pay it down than to keep the funds in your bank account to save the monthly service fees.

The following illustrations demonstrate that, when compared to conservative investment options (Guaranteed Investment Certificates or GICs for example), you can save much more by maintaining the minimum monthly balance in your account, than you would earn if you invested the amount in a GIC.

Let's look at some examples:

Example 1: : Basic Interest Rate Situation

Minimum Balance of $1,000

Mr. Tremblant has a chequing account at a bank where, if he maintains a minimum monthly balance of $1,000, his monthly fees of $6.50 are waived. As an alternative to keeping $1,000 or more in his account, Mr. Tremblant could invest these funds in a one-year GIC with an interest rate of 3%, compounded annually*.

compound interest is calculated on amount of original investment plus accumulated interest earned on prior periods. See "Principles of Saving" section for further details.

Annual savings from monthly minimum balance:	Return on a $1,000 investment in a GIC:
$6.50 × 12 = $78	$30 or 3% (before income tax)
Return: $78 ÷ $1,000 = 7.8% (after income tax)	

In the example above, it is to Mr. Tremblant's advantage to maintain the minimum monthly balance in his account until he finds an investment with after-tax returns higher than 7.8%.

Example 2: High Interest Rate Situation

Minimum Balance of $5,000

Ms. Campbell has a chequing account at a bank where, if she maintains a minimum monthly balance of $5,000, her monthly fees of $24.75 are waived. As an alternative to keeping $5,000 or more in her account, Ms. Campbell could invest these funds in a one-year GIC, with an interest rate of 5%, compounded annually.

Annual savings from monthly minimum balance: $24.75 × 12 = $297 Return: $297 ÷ $5,000 = 5.94% (after income tax)	Return on a $5,000 investment in a GIC: $250 or 5% (before income tax)

In the example above, it is to Ms. Campbell's advantage to maintain the minimum monthly balance in her account until she finds an investment with after-tax returns higher than 5.94%.

Example 3: Debt Situation

Minimum Balance of $2,000

Ms. Moffat has a chequing account at a bank where, if she maintains a minimum monthly balance of $2,000, her monthly fees of $12.75 are waived. As an alternative to keeping $2,000 or more in her account, Ms. Moffat has a credit card debt of $2,000, with an annual interest rate of 28%, compounded annually.

Annual savings from monthly minimum balance: $12.75 × 12 = $153 Return: $153 ÷ $2,000 = 7.65% (after income tax)	Interest charged on a $2,000 credit card debt: $560 or 28% (after income tax)

In the example above, it is to Ms. Moffat's advantage to pay off the credit card debt as the savings from the minimum balance are not nearly enough to offset the interest charges that are incurring on the debt at a much higher rate.

Tips to Help You Save Money

- Shop around to determine the lowest-cost service package that best suits your needs. This is essential to saving money.

- If you choose a service plan that requires you to keep a minimum balance, make sure you maintain this balance *at all times*. Otherwise, you will be charged the full monthly fee.

- Use electronic and automated services (Internet, telephone, ATMs,) whenever possible. These usually cost less than in-person branch services.

- Use your own bank's ATMs as much as possible to avoid paying unnecessary fees. Banks tend to "double dip" when you withdraw from a rival's ATM by charging an additional fee (usually $1.50) each time for "processing" at the same time as the other bank is charging you a similar fee for the same transaction. This is a high surcharge ($3) especially if you withdraw only $20 (15%) or $40 (7.5%). This does not include your standard withdrawal fee from your bank.

- Try to minimize the number of transactions you make by withdrawing one larger amount instead of several smaller ones. However, be mindful, that when people withdraw larger sums at one time, they tend to spend it quicker and on items they normally wouldn't spend on just because they have the money available.

- In stores that allow it for free, withdraw cash from your account at the same time as you make a debit card purchase (in other words, add the amount you want to withdraw to your purchase and receive the cash as change).

- If a store wants to charge you a fee for a debit card purchase, use another means of payment such as a credit card or cash, or take your business elsewhere.

Saving for Success

"I have enough money to last me the rest
of my life, unless I buy something."
– Jackie Mason

Saving money is the foundation for financial success. For most people, saving money is not easy. Clearly, it is much easier to spend money than to save it. Since saving is not comfortable, it is something we must learn to do and continuously work at. Saving money over a lifetime requires a conscious effort and an ongoing focus so that it becomes a habit.

Are you a spender or a saver? Regardless of the answer, most of us could all use a little more savings so here are some principles for saving money.

1. **Know how much you make and how much you spend.**

   The starting point for any financial goal is to understand your spending patterns. Track your expenses. Just knowing how much you spend and where you spend your money sets the foundation for a sound financial future. (See the "Budgeting" section for guidance, later in this book.)

2. Save first, spend later.

Now is the time to get started. Start an automatic savings plan with your bank. Arrange to have money automatically come out of your bank account or off your paycheque. Most people spend first and try to save what little they have left over. The best plan is to save first and then spend what you have left over. Usually there are no fees for an automatic savings plan.

3. Understand the benefits of compound interest over simple interest.

There are two common types of interest – simple and compound. Compound interest occurs when interest is earned and it is added to the principal (i.e. original amount invested). Future interest is then earned on the principal and the past interest earned. The other option is simple interest where interest is *not* added to the principal. Future interest is earned on the principal only.

Compound interest is the type that will grow your money faster. The key to understanding compound interest is that once you get enough money working for you, you then no longer have to work for money.

How Interest Works

Here's an example of the difference between simple and compound interest on a savings account:

<u>Simple Interest</u>

Simple interest is calculated by multiplying the original deposit ("the principal" - e.g. $1000) by the interest rate (e.g. 5%) by the number of periods over the life of the deposit (e.g. 24 months).

For example, using the figures above, our $1000 principal would be at 5% per year, over a period of 2 years (as opposed to 24 months). The calculation would be 1000 x 0.05 x 2 (principal x interest x term) = 100. The amount of simple interest that we would receive on this principal over the two year term would be $100.

Compound Interest

Compound interest relates to charges the bank must pay not just on the original amount deposited, as in simple interest, but also on any interest earned in previous terms. To illustrate the difference between compounding interest and simple interest, consider the following very simplified scenario of a $1000 deposit invested at 10% over 2 years (assuming no withdrawals are taken until the end of the term):

Example of Simple vs. Compound Interest on a $1000 investment over 2 years

Simple Interest:

1st year	$ 1,000	x	1 year	x	10%	= $ 100 interest
2nd year	$ 1,000	x	1 year	x	10%	= $ 100 interest

Total   **Interest:**   **$ 200**

Total of the original loan amount plus interest =   **$ 1,200**

In this scenario, the total amount of interest paid over the 2 year period would be   **$200**

Compound Interest:

1st year	$ 1,000	x	1 year	x	10%	= $ 100 interest
2nd year	$ 1,100	x	1 year	x	10%	= $ 110 interest

Total   **Interest:**   **$ 210**

Total of the original investment amount plus interest =   **$ 1,210**

In this scenario, with interest compounded annually, the total amount of interest earned is **$210**

4. **Start saving sooner than later.**

The sooner you start saving, the more you will have later based on the compound interest example above. Don't procrastinate! It's never too late to start.

5. **Something is better than nothing.**

How much should you save? The amount is less important than getting a savings plan started soon. You've got to start the habit. Never let any hurdles get in the way of getting you started. Remember something is better than nothing and more is better than less.

6. **Stay disciplined.**

Saving money is hard work. It is so easy to get lured into spending your money on the next gadget. Saving money requires both effort and discipline. But the rewards are worth it!

How to Open a Bank Account

Now that you know about different types of bank accounts, you are ready to open an account of your own. Where can you do this and what documentation do you need? Firstly, before you go to your nearest bank branch, you should be aware of your rights.

Opening An Account: Your Rights

Under Canadian law, you have certain rights when you are dealing with a bank. You have the right to a personal bank account, even if:

- You don't have a job;

- You don't have money to put in the account right away; or,

- You have been bankrupt.

What do you have to do to open an account?

To open an account, you have to go to the bank in-person, and show the bank some acceptable identification (I.D.). You must use **original** I.D., not a photocopy.

What identification (I.D.) do you need?

There are different combinations of I.D. you can use. You have three choices. You must have at least one piece of I.D. from List #1 (below).

List #1:

Show two pieces of I.D. from this list. If you don't have two pieces of I.D. , select one of the other choices.

- Canadian driver's licence.

- Valid Canadian passport.

- Canadian birth certificate.

- Social Insurance Number (SIN) card.

- Certificate of Indian Status.

- Provincial or territorial health insurance card (except in Ontario, P.E.I. or Manitoba).

- Certificate of Canadian Citizenship or Certification of Naturalization.

- Permanent Resident card or a Citizenship and Immigration Canada form IMM 1000, IMM 1442, or IMM 5292.

Show one piece of I.D. from previous list and one piece of I.D. from this list (below).

- Employee I.D. card with a photo, from a known employer.

- Debit card or bank card with your name and signature on it.

- Canadian credit card with your name and signature on it.

- Canadian National Institute for the Blind (CNIB) client card with your photo and signature on it.

- Valid foreign passport.

You can also show other types of I.D. To find out what they are, call FCAC toll-free at: 1-866-461-3222.

List #3:

Show one piece of I.D. from List #1 and have someone whom the bank knows confirm that you are who you say you are.

Information you must receive when you open your account:

When you open an account, a bank must provide you with the following information in **writing** (either at or before the time the account is opened):

- A copy of the account agreement.

- For an account that pays interest, the rate of interest on the account and how it will be calculated (this rule doesn't apply to an account opened with a balance in excess of $150,000).

- All of the charges that apply to the account.

- How you will be notified of any increase in those charges, and of any new charges to the account.

- The bank's procedures if you have a complaint about any charges on your account.

- The bank's policies with respect to hold periods on deposits.

When can a bank refuse to open a personal bank account?

A bank can legitimately refuse to open a personal bank account for you if:

- The bank has reasonable grounds to believe that you'll use the account to break the law or commit fraud; and/or

- You've committed a crime or fraud against a financial institution during the past seven years; and/or

- It has reasonable grounds to believe that you intentionally provided false information when you opened the account; and/or

- It has reasonable grounds to believe that opening the account would expose its employees or customers to physical harm, harassment or abuse; and/or

- You do not agree to let the bank verify if the four circumstances mentioned above can apply to you and to verify the pieces of identification that you present to the bank; and/ or

- You can't provide acceptable identification.

What if the bank won't open an account for you?

Ask the bank for a letter saying that it will not open an account for you. The bank must give you this letter. By law, the bank must also tell you how to contact the Financial Consumer Agency of Canada (FCAC). http://www.fcac-acfc.gc.ca/

Tell the bank you want to make a complaint. By law, all banks must have a complaint-handling process.

What if the bank wants to check your credit report?

When you ask to open a personal bank account, the bank often contacts a credit-reporting agency to get a copy of your credit report. Credit-reporting agencies are organizations that maintain credit reports for millions of Canadian consumers. Banks can use your credit report to double-check the information you provide them. Your file will show and confirm to the bank information such as the following:

- Your personal identification (your name, address, birth date, etc.).
- Your employment history.
- Your current and past debts.
- Whether you pay your bills on time.
- Your bankruptcy history, and any judgments and/or third-party collections, if any.

Your file will also indicate to the bank any confirmed misuse or irregularities related to your address, social insurance number or telephone number.

This information will help the bank determine the reasons for refusal that apply to you. It will also help the bank decide what you can do with your account (see the next section: "How the bank uses your credit information").

By law, if the bank contacts a credit-reporting agency to obtain information about you, it can't normally use this information to deny you an account. It can only do so if the information contained in your credit file provides the bank with reasonable grounds to believe that you have been involved in dishonest or fraudulent activity. The fact that you have a poor credit rating or have declared bankruptcy in the past is not, by itself, a valid reason for refusing to open an account for you.

How the bank uses your credit information

The bank may use the information it obtains from the credit bureau check to help it decide what you can do with your personal bank account. The information will help the bank:

- Establish how much money you can withdraw from your account through an automated banking machine; and

- Determine whether you will be able to deposit cheques at an automated banking machine and how long the bank will place a "hold" on the money you deposit into your account by cheque; and

- Decide whether to provide you with a chequing account or a basic savings account.

Thinking of Opening a Tax-Free Savings Account (TFSA)?

What is a Tax-Free Savings Account (TFSA)?

A Tax-Free Savings Account (TFSA) is similar to a savings account. It allows you to earn interest without paying taxes on it. Interest earned in a standard savings or investment account is taxable.

Starting in 2009, Canadian residents aged 18 or older who have a valid Social Insurance Number (SIN) can contribute up to a set limit each year to a TFSA. **The key benefit is that you do not have to pay taxes on earnings within the account (including interest, dividends or capital gains) or on money you withdraw from the TFSA.**

What are the annual contribution limits?

As of 2009, you can contribute up to $5,000 annually to a TFSA. If you do not contribute one year or contribute less than the maximum, you can carry forward the unused amount to future years.

If you go over your annual contribution limit, **you will be taxed 1 percent a month on the highest excess amount** for that month until you remove it from the TFSA.

Where can I open a TFSA?

You can open a TFSA at most financial institutions, such as banks, credit unions, trust and loan companies, and life insurance companies.

What investments can I hold in a TFSA?

Your TFSA can contain the following types of investments:

- Cash
- Guaranteed Investment Certificates (GICs)
- Government and Corporate Bonds
- Mutual Funds
- Publicly Traded Securities/Stocks

What happens when I withdraw from a TFSA?

If you withdraw money from your TFSA, your annual contribution limit increases by the amount withdrawn – **but only in the following calendar year**. For example, suppose you withdraw $500 from your TFSA in 2009. In 2010, $500 will be added to your contribution room and your new limit for 2010 will be $5,500.

Key features of a TFSA

A TFSA has the following key features:

- Earnings in the account grow tax-free.
- You can take money out without being taxed on it. The money you withdraw can be used any way you like.
- You can carry forward the unused contribution room, increasing the allowable limit in future years.
- Contributions to the account will not reduce your income taxes like an RRSP can.
- There is a maximum contribution limit set for each calendar year, starting with $5,000 in 2009. You can only contribute up to that limit, plus any unused contribution room from previous years.
- If you go over your annual contribution limit, you will be taxed 1 percent a month on the highest excess amount for that month until you remove it from the TFSA.

Low-Cost Bank Accounts

What is a low-cost bank account?

A low-cost account is a bank account that costs a maximum of $4.00 per month and includes the following features:

- No charge for deposits.
- The use of a debit card.
- Cheque-writing privileges.
- A free periodic statement of your account that shows you all of the money that came out of and went into your account during the month.
- Eight to 15 debit transactions per month — at least two of which can be made in the branch.

Where can you open a low-cost bank account?

The following eight banks offer low-cost accounts:

- CIBC
- HSBC Bank Canada
- Laurentian Bank
- National Bank
- Royal Bank
- Scotiabank
- TD Canada Trust
- BMO Bank of Montreal

Under Canadian Federal law — subject to certain types of identification — anyone can open an account with a bank. However, other deposit-taking institutions, such as credit unions, are regulated provincially and may have different requirements.

Some questions to ask when shopping around for a low-cost bank account:

- Are there branches of the financial institution close to where you go most often? (for example, near your home, work or school)
- How many transactions will you make on a monthly basis?
  Make sure you know how many transactions you are allowed to make each month with a low-cost account so you don't go over this limit and find you have to pay extra fees.
- What kind of identification (I.D.) will you need to open a low-cost account?

Checklist - some things to think about

- What is more important to you: convenience or low fees?

- How do you like to do your banking? Do you want to make your banking transactions in-person only? (This is called in-branch banking.) Self-serve only? (by doing your banking through the automated teller/banking machines [ATMs/ABMs], phone or Internet)? Perhaps you need a combination of in-branch banking and self-serve banking.

- Where do you plan to do your banking? If you want to make some or all of your banking transactions in-person or at an ATM, are the bank branches or ATMs conveniently located so you can do the majority of your banking at that institution?

- There are extra fees you will have to pay if you do your banking transactions at the ATMs of another financial institution. Do you know what these extra charges are? Do you know the locations of the ATMs of your own financial institution? Get to know where they are so you can use these ATMs instead to avoid paying additional charges.

- If you want to do some in-branch transactions, do the branches have convenient business hours?

- Does your financial institution offer a low-fee or no-fee account?

- Could you benefit from a student or youth's service package with minimal or no fees?

- Does the financial institution have service packages that include *all* the types of transactions you will need? Transactions include withdrawing money from your account, transferring money from and into your account, writing cheques, paying bills or using your debit card.

- Are specialized services (such as certified cheques, money orders, bank drafts overdraft protection, cheque return, safe deposit box, traveller's cheques) important to you? If so, it may be more beneficial to look for a service package that includes those services than to pay a fee each time you use them.

- To choose the right service package, you will have to figure out how many times you think you will need to make a withdrawal, a transfer, a bill payment, a direct payment or write a cheque, each month. How many transactions will your service package allow you to make each month? This is called the "monthly transaction limit". (See the exercise: "Chequing Plans: Which Would You Rather?" earlier in the book.)

- If you go over this "monthly transaction limit", there may be a cost for each additional transaction you make. Do you know what you will have to pay for each additional transaction?

- Depending on your service package, sometimes the financial institution will not charge you the monthly fee, especially if you keep a specified minimum amount of money in your account. Do you know what the minimum amount would be so you can avoid paying this fee?

Payday Loans

What are payday loans?

Payday loans are paycheque cashing stores that charge a fee to cash your cheque. Payday lenders typically extend loans based on a percentage of your net pay (i.e. after taxes and deductions) until your next payday (generally within two weeks or less). You provide the payday lender with a post-dated cheque or authorize a direct withdrawal for the value of the loan plus any interest or fees charged.

Some payday lenders will cash your post-dated cheque or process the direct withdrawal on the due date of the loan. Others will require that you repay the loan in cash on or before the due date, and may charge an additional fee if the loan is not repaid on time. If there are insufficient funds in your account, you may also be required to pay a return fee to the payday lender and/or a non-sufficient funds (NSF) fee to his/her bank. In this instance, you may have the option of "rolling over" the loan – that is, taking out another payday loan to pay off the original loan – for an additional fee.

Pay day loan companies are under scrutiny for their excessive interest rates and fees.

If you calculate the rate of interest charged on payday loan transactions using the definitions and methods specified in the Criminal Code where exceeding 60% annual interest is not allowed, some payday loan companies appear to be charging criminal rates of interest. The following table illustrates this point by showing the details of an actual payday loan transaction.

Sample Payday Loan Transaction	
Value of the payday loan advanced on 27 September 2009	$400.00
Amount paid by you on 14 October 2009	$451.28
Term of the loan	17 days
Breakdown of amount paid by you:	
Principal	$400.00
Interest	$8.64
Per item fee	$9.99
Cheque-cashing fees (7.99% of principal and interest)	$32.65
Effective annual rate of interest	1,242%

Consumer advocacy groups have raised concerns regarding what they view as the "predatory" lending practices of some payday lenders. While the federal and provincial governments are reviewing potential legislation to standardize the industry, the industry currently remains unregulated.

As of November 1, 2009, the Payday Loans Regulation legislation was put in place in British Columbia to:

- ⊘ Cap the maximum charges for short term loans to 23% (including interests and fees).
- ⊘ Allow the borrower to cancel the loan by the end of the following day of signing the agreement without paying any charge.
- ⊘ Allow only 1 loan per borrower at a time.
- ⊘ Restrict the ability for lenders to access to borrower's bank or employer.
- ⊘ Restrict lenders from lending more than 50 per cent of a borrower's take-home pay.
- ⊘ Prohibit lenders from demanding repayment before the borrower's next payday.
- ⊘ Require all lenders to register and be regulated under the Business Practices and Consumer Protection Authority.

As of October 18, 2010, Manitoba introduced changes to its Payday Loans Regulation.

- ⊘ The new maximum rate that can be charged for a payday loan is $17 per $100.
- ⊘ The maximum amount of a loan can only be 30 percent of a person's next net pay.
- ⊘ All fees are to be included in the cost of credit, whether or not they are optional;
- ⊘ The maximum fee for a replacement loan is five per cent;
- ⊘ Lenders, including brokers, must be licensed and bonded;
- ⊘ Written consent is required for a lender to verify a borrower's employment; and
- ⊘ Lenders cannot make unauthorized withdrawals from a borrower's account or use rewards or incentives to entice borrowers to get a loan.

Manitoba's rate is the lowest in the country among provinces that effectively allow payday loans.

Here's how the rates compare to the rest in Canada:

Province	Maximum that can be charged on the principal of a $100 loan	Maximum annual percentage rate for a 12-day loan
Nova Scotia (in force)	$31	943%
British Columbia (in force)	$23	700%
Alberta (in force)	$23	700%
Saskatchewan (announced)	$23	700%
Ontario (in force)	$21	639%
Manitoba	$17	517%

Therefore, it is recommended that due to fees and interest rates, pay day lenders are an expensive choice and are not recommended as a regular means to obtain cash.

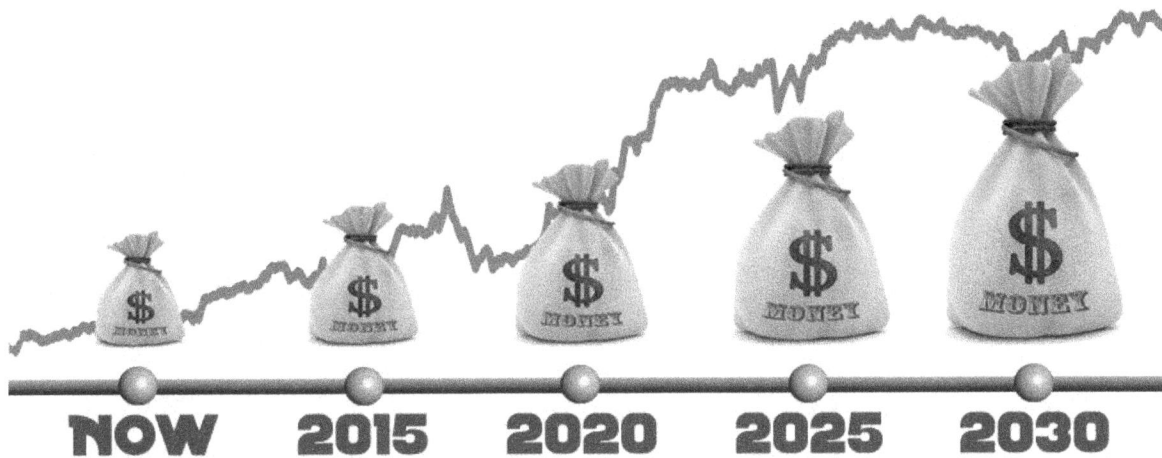

NOW   2015   2020   2025   2030

Investing in your Future

Once you have your money saved, what should you do with it? There are many different options that have different risk and rewards levels.

Standard Investments

Investment	Advantages	Disadvantages
Canada Savings Bonds – Government bond that can be purchased at most banks and trust companies. (A bond is a commitment to pay a specified interest rate.)	☑ Safest investment ☑ Smallest amounts (i.e. as low as $100) ☑ Rate of return known at time of purchase ☑ Can be cashed at any time with some interest paid, makes great emergency funds	☑ Interest is not as high as some other investments ☑ Interest is taxed ☑ Cannot be sold to other investors

Savings account – a bank account that pays interest for saving money	☑ Safe, insured by government ☑ Pays interest ☑ Can deposit or withdraw money at any time ☑ Bank keeps record of amounts saved	☑ Interest rates are lower than other investments ☑ Interest is taxed ☑ Interest rates are not guaranteed, they fluctuate.
GIC (Guaranteed Investment Certificate) – A certificate guaranteeing a fixed rate of interest on the money you deposit	☑ Safe, insured by government ☑ Higher interest than savings account ☑ Interest rate is same for 1-5 years	☑ Money must be left in for full period (1-5 years) to get full rate of interest ☑ Interest is taxed ☑ Cannot be sold to another person ☑ May be penalty for withdrawing money early
Mutual Funds – A collection of different financial investments	☑ May be safer than buying stocks ☑ Mutual fund is overseen by experienced manager ☑ Allows diversification ☑ May reduce risk	☑ Market value goes up and down ☑ Future rate of return is uncertain ☑ There may be penalties if you withdraw your money early
Stocks – Part ownership of a company	☑ Potential for higher return on investment in market ☑ As an investor, you direct your money to a specific company of interest to you ☑ Can track the value of the investment daily on the Internet or newspaper	☑ Rate of return is uncertain ☑ May not be able to get cash from sale of stocks when needed ☑ Pay commission on trading ☑ Can be complex ☑ Many factors can impact stock values

Long Term Investment Plans

There are a few government programs that encourage specific savings that can provide tax benefits.

Program	Tax Benefits/Deferrals
RRSP stands for **Registered Retirement Savings Plan**. An RRSP is a government approved plan through which you save money for retirement. RRSPs were designed to encourage and help Canadians save for their retirement.	The contributions you make to your RRSP are **tax deductible**, reducing your taxable income. Your RRSP contributions offer a deferral of tax because the government allows you to push a portion of your taxable income to a future year such as when you retire when you are expected to be in a lower tax bracket. The income earned in an RRSP is tax sheltered. This means that the investments inside your RRSP will not be taxed as they grow each year. Over time, this significantly increases your earnings. Taxes on your RRSP investments are not paid until you withdraw funds. By that time you should be retired and your annual income may likely be much less and so will your tax rate.
RRIF stands for **Registered Retirement Income Fund**. A RRIF is a financial product that is funded with the money earned in your Registered Retirement Savings Plan (RRSP). RRIFs are designed to provide you with an income stream during your retirement years.	Your RRSP can be transferred **tax-free** to a RRIF to establish a source of retirement income. Much like a RRSP, the income earned in an RRIF is tax sheltered. This means that the investments inside your RRIF will not be taxed as they grow each year. However, unlike a RRSP, you must withdraw a minimum annual payment set by the government. At 71, it is mandatory to either withdraw all funds from an RRSP plan or convert the RRSP to an RRIF

RESP stands for **Registered Education Savings Plan**. An RESP is a plan through which your parents (or grandparents) can save money for a child's (under the age of 18) post-secondary educational expenses.

RESP savings can be used to pay for educational expenses such as tuition, books, and living expenses.

Unlike RRSPs, contributions made to an RESP are **not tax deductible.** However, the contributions grow tax-free in the plan.

Regardless of what your family income is, under this program the government pays up to 20% of annual contributions made to all eligible RESPs.

This enables each beneficiary to receive up to a maximum of $500 per year with a lifetime limit of $7,200 from the government.

If the student elects to not attend a post-secondary institution, any accumulated interest may be withdrawn by the contributor and is taxed as income plus 20% unless it is rolled into a registered retirement savings plan (RRSP). The original amount contributed to the RESP will also go back to the contributor unless it can be transferred to a sibling who has contribution room in his/her RESP.

Ways to Pay

The days of "cash only" are behind us. With so many different ways to pay for expenses available to us, it can be confusing as to which way is best. Here is a chart of the advantages and disadvantages of the most accepted types of payments.

Payment Methods

Payment Method	Advantages	Disadvantages
Cash – Paper currency and coins.	☑ Always accepted ☑ You know how much you have ☑ Tangible	☒ Can be easily stolen/lost ☒ Doesn't gain in value ☒ Not convenient to carry large amounts for large purchases (house, car, etc.)
Cheques – Financial instrument instructing a financial institution to pay a specific amount of a specific currency from a specific account held in the writer's name with that institution.	☑ You don't have to carry a wad of money so it is physically safe ☑ You can't spend more than you have in your account	☒ Not always accepted ☒ Need ID to use (hassle) ☒ Handwritten ☒ Signature can be forged ☒ No trust as you can't give someone a signed cheque to fill in amount ☒ Sometimes needs to be

Payment Method	Advantages	Disadvantages
		certified for large purchases so you need to go to the bank to use in this case
Debit Card – Plastic card which provides an alternative payment method to cash when making purchases. Funds are withdrawn immediately from the owner's bank account.	☑ Convenient ☑ Safe (if you keep your PIN confidential) ☑ Can't spend more than you have in your account	☒ May forget your PIN ☒ Card can be lost ☒ Card can be demagnetized and needs replacement ☒ If ATM system down, you cannot access your money ☒ Bank and user fees for transactions
Credit Card – Entitles its holder to buy goods and services based on the holder's promise to pay for these goods and services. They allow the consumers to maintain a balance, at the cost of having interest charged.	☑ Convenient ☑ Access to higher amounts ☑ Earn credit rating ☑ Buy now, pay later ☑ No transaction charges ☑ Some have reward point system	☒ Easy to overspend ☒ High interest rate ☒ Lose credit rating if you miss any payments ☒ Annual fees ☒ Potential for fraud
Electronic Funds Transfer (EFT) – Transfer of money electronically through your online banking account to pay bills online.	☑ Convenient ☑ Transfer money immediately ☑ Safe, little security risk ☑ No transaction charges ☑ Private ☑ Online record of transaction	☒ Must have access to internet ☒ There may be a delay of several days before bill is actually paid ☒ There may be a monthly charge for internet access ☒ Have to keep password secret
Stored value Cards / Gift Cards – Issued by retailers or banks to be used as an alternative to a non-monetary gift.	☑ Gives a bonus for each transaction ☑ No cost	☒ Must use at the issuing business ☒ May be hard to claim rewards ☒ Potential loss of privacy ☒ Not secure ☒ Card can be lost

✍ Exercise: Which should you use?

Which version of payment should you use? (Select the best method. In some cases, there may be more than one option.)

Buying gum and milk at the convenience store.	Cash? Cheque? Debit Card? Credit Card? EFT?
Taking your best friend out to dinner for his/her birthday.	Cash? Cheque? Debit Card? Credit Card? EFT?
Buying groceries for the week.	Cash? Cheque? Debit Card? Credit Card? EFT?
Buying gas.	Cash? Cheque? Debit Card? Credit Card? EFT?
Paying the hydro bill.	Cash? Cheque? Debit Card? Credit Card? EFT?
Making a donation to charity.	Cash? Cheque? Debit Card? Credit Card? EFT?

Paying your rent.	Cash? Cheque? Debit Card? Credit Card? EFT?
Getting your car washed at the annual charity car wash.	Cash? Cheque? Debit Card? Credit Card? EFT?
Going to McDonald's.	Cash? Cheque? Debit Card? Credit Card? EFT?
Buying an iPod.	Cash? Cheque? Debit Card? Credit Card? EFT?

See Appendix D for answers.

Give Credit Cards Where Credit is Due

Shopping for the Best Credit Card

In addition to looking at fees and interest (also known as the annual percentage rate or "APR") that you will be charged, consider your lifestyle and past payment history when shopping for a credit card. Factors you may want to consider include:

- A fixed (i.e. set-in-stone) vs. a variable rate of interest. Most cards use a variable rate which can change monthly depending on the prime rate issued by the Bank of Canada. A fixed rate will not fluctuate as the prime rate changes (although a credit card company reserves the right to change their rate with notice to its customers).

- The minimum payment that you are required to make.

- The maximum amount that you can borrow without being penalized with an over-the-limit fee.

- Fees such as an annual fee, late payment charges and interest rates on cash advances.

- Circumstances when the credit card company can change the conditions of your agreement. Sometimes a credit card company will send you a multi-page pamphlet of fine print notifying you of numerous changes to their agreement with you. Some changes may include days you have to pay without interest penalties, changes in the reward plan (e.g. Air Miles), or changes in how interest is calculated. Their obligation is to notify you. They do not need to receive your consent or acknowledgement of receipt to proceed with the changes. These changes are rarely to your benefit.

- How the company calculates the finance charge. Is it based on the average daily balance, the balance at the beginning of the billing cycle, or another amount?

- A low introductory interest rate, if offered. When is the rate likely to increase? What is the new rate likely to be?

- Incentives such as cash rebates on purchases, purchase protection and frequent flyer miles.

- Your prior payment history. If you typically pay off your balance every month, the APR may be less of an issue than getting cash back with a purchase.

Credit Card Statements

Understanding your credit card statement is imperative if you regularly spend on your credit card and need to follow a tight budget. To many people, reading a credit card statement is fairly straightforward, yet for newcomers there may be a couple of features that need to be clarified. The key features of your credit card statement include:

Prepared For			Account Number		Closing Date
John A. Smith			3733 **XXXXXX XXXX**	**1**	Sep 09, 2010

	Previous Balance		**3**	$815.33	Credit Limit	**9**	$18,250.00
LESS	Payments & Credits		**5**	$300.00	Available Credit Limit		$17,259.91
PLUS	New Charges/Adjustments	inc. Interest, if any		$474.76	Available Cash Limit		$3,650.00
EQUALS	New Balance		**10**	$990.09			

Payment Period Remaining

Minimum Amount Due on Sep 30, 2010	**2**	**$30.00** If each month you pay the Minimum Amount Due only
Statement includes payments and charges received by Sep 9, 2010	**4**	7 Year(s) 2 Month(s)

Your Transactions

Transaction Date	Posting Date	Details		Amount ($)
Aug 18	Aug 18	PAYMENT RECEIVED - THANK YOU Reference AT102300005000010009231	**5**	-300.00
Total of Payment Activity				**-300.00**
Aug 26	Aug 27	IFAW INC		5.00
Total of new transactions			**8**	**5.00**
Aug 9	Aug 11	TORONTO PARKING AUTH		12.00
Aug 10	Aug 11	RBC GENERAL		195.82
Aug 13	Aug 14	CLARKE HUSKY		58.50
Aug 17	Aug 18	PETSMART		38.39
Aug 23	Aug 25	AMAZON.COM		62.14
Aug 29	Aug 30	COSTCO		96.40
Total of new transactions				**463.25**

Transaction Date	Posting Date	Details		Amount ($)
OTHER ACCOUNT TRANSACTIONS				
Sep 9	Sep 9	INTEREST	**6**	6.51
Total of other account transactions				**6.51**

Account Number		3733 **XXXX XXX**
New Balance	**10**	$990.09
Minimum Due	**4**	$30.00
Payment Due Date		Sep 30, 2010

Amount Paid ($)

Category		Daily Periodic Rate 31 Billing days this Period	Interest	Current Annual Interest Rate	Annual Interest Rates		
					Preferred	Standard	Basic
Purchases	12	0.0356%	$6.51	12.99%	12.99 %	21.99 %	25.99 %
Funds Advance	11	0.0548%	$0.00	19.99%	19.99 %	21.99 %	25.99 %
Amex Cheques/Balance Transfers		0.0356%	$0.00	12.99%	12.99 %	21.99 %	25.99 %
			$6.51				

#1 – The Statement Period

Knowing this period of time is important to take advantage of your "interest free" period (the time span between transaction date and the payment due date which can be up to 55 days). So if you know that your statement date is always on the 9th of a month, it is advantageous to you to delay a purchase to the 10th or 11th of the month to get the maximum interest free period. These later purchases won't show up until the statement for the following month and therefore won't be included in your current card balance due.

Sometimes banks will promote a 55 day interest free period. It is misleading as it meant to give you the erroneous impression that all your purchases are eligible for 55 days of no interest. So when does the 55 day interest free period actually apply? What it actually applies to is the '55 days' from the start of your last statement period, till it's 'Payment due date' (2). From the statement above, this is a grace period of 53 days between the 27th of February and the 20th of April. If you made a purchase on April 16th for example, you only effectively have 4 interest free days on your purchase.

#2 – Payment Due Date

This is the date you must pay at least the 'minimum amount due' (3) for your current credit card statement. If you do not pay at least the minimum repayment, your credit card rating will be affected and you will be charged a late payment fee (usually around $10-40 depending on your bank).

#3 – Previous Balance

This is the amount that was not paid from the previous month's statement. You will be incurring interest on this amount daily until it is paid off.

#4 – Minimum Amount Due & Due Date

The Minimum Amount Due is also known as your "minimum repayment". This figure is often 2 - 5% of your balance or $10 - 30, generally whichever is higher applies. Try to avoid paying only the minimum repayment unless absolutely necessary, as it can take years to pay off balances as low as $500 (thus accumulating significant interest over that period of time).

The due date is very important to understand. If you don't make even the minimum payment by this date, you will risk your credit card being rejected for future purchases and your credit rating being negatively affected.

#5 – Payments/Refunds

This is the total amount of all your repayments made towards your credit card in your statement period to date.

#6 – Interest Charges

This is the amount of interest that you have been charged on your outstanding balance from your previous statement. Any time that you do not pay your balance in full on time, you will accumulate interest charges at the specified daily rate. These amounts can add up substantially so you should try to pay off as much of your credit card balance each month as you can realistically afford.

#7 – Rewards Program Earning (not available in the example above)

Many credit cards include "rewards" or "loyalty" programs such as Air Miles, cashback, CAA dollars, and so on. These programs are built into the card features as an enticement for you to use that card. This section shows you how many "points" you have earned towards that program.

#8 – Transactions

This area lists all your transactions, including the date of purchase, transaction reference code, what was purchased and how much it cost. Make sure that you review this thoroughly for charges that you did not make. If you find such charges, contact the credit card company within 30 days to file a complaint. If you act after 30 days, the credit card company may refuse to process the investigation. Check with your credit card company on what their policy and procedure is in this situation. Most companies will have this information posted on their website somewhere (usually under the section on how to file a dispute).

#9 – Credit Limit & Credit Available.

The credit limit is the maximum amount that you are allowed to charge to your card. If you exceed this amount, you will be charged a substantial penalty and your card may be disabled. The limit is comprised of overdue balances, new purchases, interest charges and penalties.

The credit available is the result of your credit limit minus your outstanding balance. It indicates how much credit is available before you reach your credit limit.

#10 – Account Balance

How much you currently owe on your credit card. If you have put more money on your card than your balance, this figure will be displayed as negative.

#11 – Purchase / Cash Advance Rate

These are your standard annual percentage rates (APR) on purchases and cash advances (i.e. cash withdrawals).

#12 – Daily Rate

Although interest rates are given as a yearly figure, this is the real figure which applies to your transactions. This is how much interest will accumulate on your purchases/cash advances each day. You can find this figure by dividing your annual rate by 365.

Key Credit Card Terms

If you don't understand the language, credit card offers and statements could lead you into deep debt -- or at least frantic frustration. For the clarification on the fine print, here's what these frequently used credit card terms mean.

Average daily balance

This is the method by which most credit cards calculate your payment due. An average daily balance is determined by adding each day's balance and then dividing that total by the number of days in a billing cycle.

For example:

Let's say throughout the month, your balances are:

Dates of the month	Balance
1st to 10th inclusive (10 days)	$100.00
11th to 19th inclusive (9 days)	$250.00
20th to 25th inclusive (6 days)	$200.00
26th to 31st inclusive (6 days)	$400.00

If you average totals for each day over the month (i.e. $100 x 10 + $250 x 9 + $200 x 6 + $400 x 6 = $6850.00 divided by 31 days), the average daily balance is $220.97.

The average daily balance is then multiplied by a card's monthly rate, which is calculated by dividing the annual percentage rate by 12.

For example, a card with an annual rate of 18 percent would have a monthly periodic rate of 1.5 percent (18% divided by 12 equals 1.5%). If that card had a $500 average daily balance it would yield a monthly finance charge of $7.50 (1.5% x $500 = 7.50).

In our example above, the monthly charge would be $3.31 ($220.97 x 1.5%).

✒ Exercise: Monthly Charges

Try to figure out what the monthly charge would be based an *annual* interest rate of 28% on the following figures: (see Appendix D for the answer.)

Dates of the month	Balance
1st to 7th inclusive (7 days)	$ 500.00
8th to 14th inclusive (7 days)	$ 750.00
15th to 22nd inclusive (8 days)	$ 900.00
23rd to 31st inclusive (9 days)	$1,400.00

Annual Percentage Rate (APR)

A yearly rate of interest that banks charge to advance / loan money to clients whether you are borrowing cash (loans or cash advance on your credit card), charging items on a credit card, financing a car or getting a mortgage.

Balance Transfer

The process of moving an unpaid credit card debt from one card to another. Credit card companies sometimes offer "teaser" rates to encourage its customers to move the balances that they may have on other cards to their credit card at a lower rate for a specified period of time. For example, you may receive a letter or credit card "cheques" that give you a substantially lower rate (e.g. 2.99%) for six months if you transfer any outstanding amounts from any other credit card accounts. These can be advantageous as long as you understand how long the rate will last, what the rate will increase to after the specified term and if there is a service fee to make the transfer.

Cash-Advance Fee

A fee charged by the bank for using credit cards to obtain cash. This fee can be a flat per-transaction fee (e.g. $5 per withdrawal) or a percentage of the amount of the cash advance. For example, the fee may be expressed as follows: "2% / $10". This means that the cash advance fee will be either the greater of 2% of the cash advance amount or $10, whichever is higher.

The banks may limit the fee that can be charged to a specific dollar amount. The cost of a cash advance is also higher because there is generally no grace period. Interest starts being calculated from the moment the money is withdrawn.

Cardholder Agreement

The written statement that gives the terms and conditions of a credit card account. It must include the Annual Percentage Rate, the monthly minimum payment formula, annual fee if applicable, and the cardholder's rights in billing disputes. Changes in the cardholder agreement may be made, with advance written notice, at any time by the issuer.

Finance Charge

The fee for using a credit card is comprised of interest costs and other fees.

Grace Period

If the credit card user does not carry a balance, the grace period is the interest-free time a lender allows between the transaction date and the billing date. The standard grace period is usually between 20 and 30 days. If there is no grace period, finance charges will accumulate the moment a purchase is made with the credit card. People who carry a balance on their credit cards have no grace period.

Minimum Payment

The minimum amount a cardholder can pay to keep the account from going into default (i.e. your card is cancelled, collection agencies harass you and your credit rating is negatively affected). Some card issuers will set a high minimum if they are uncertain of the cardholder's ability to pay. Most card issuers require a minimum payment of two percent of the outstanding balance.

Over-The-Limit Fee

A fee charged for exceeding the credit limit on the card. So, if your credit limit is $5,000 and your balance creeps to $5,100, you will be charged a sizable penalty that will build until you lower your balance. In this case, a business may reject (or even cut up) your card during your transaction which can be both inconvenient and humiliating.

Periodic Rate

The interest rate described in relation to a specific amount of time. The monthly periodic rate, for example, is the interest charged per month; the daily periodic rate is the cost of interest charged per day.

Pre-Approved

A "pre-approved" credit card offer suggests that a potential customer has passed a preliminary credit-information screening. A credit card company can reject the customers it has invited with "pre-approved" junk mail if it doesn't like the applicant's credit rating.

Secured Card

It is a credit card that a cardholder guarantees with a savings account as a backup to ensure payment of the outstanding balance if the cardholder defaults on payments. It is used by people new to credit, or people trying to rebuild their poor credit ratings.

Teaser Rate

Often called the introductory rate, it is the below-market interest rate offered to entice customers to switch credit cards. For example, you may get mail encouraging you to transfer your balances from your other credit cards at a low rate of 2.99% for 10 months.

Variable Interest Rate

Percentage that a credit card owner or loan borrower pays for the use of money. The rate moves up or down periodically based on changes in other interest rates such as the Bank of Canada rate and/or bank interest rates.

Quiz: (courtesy of Financial Consumer Agency of Canada)

1. Last month, your credit card balance was zero. This month, your statement shows that you made a $500 purchase. If you can pay off only $400 by the due date indicated on your statement, you will be charged interest only on the $100 left to pay. True or False?

2. You make a purchase on your new credit card at the beginning of the month. Mid-month, you request a balance transfer - at a low promotional rate - from other credit cards to your new one. When you make a credit card payment, this payment is first applied to your purchase, since it occurred before the balance transfer. True or False?

3. All credit card issuers have the same rule: if you pay off your credit card bill in full by the due date indicated on your statement, you won't be charged interest on any purchases that appear on that statement. True or False?

4. You won't pay interest on a cash advance as long as you pay your credit card bill in full by the due date indicated on your statement. True or False?

5. All credit cards have the same grace period. True or False?

6. Most credit card issuers have formal policies in place to protect cardholders against unauthorized transactions on their accounts. True or False?

7. If you frequently pay your credit card just a couple of days after the due date, this won't affect your credit rating. True or False?

8. Credit rating agencies will charge you a fee for sending you a copy of your credit report by mail. True or False?

9. Your January statement, dated January 31, shows that you owe $550 because of a purchase you've been carrying over since October. Your next credit card payment is due on February 15. If you pay $550 on February 13, you won't owe anything more. True or False?

10. A credit card issuer can increase the administration fee it charges for a cash advance without telling you in advance. True or False?

(see the next page for the answers)

Answers:

1 –False - It is a common myth to think that you will pay interest only on the amount left to pay (also called the outstanding amount) on your credit card bill. If you don't pay in full by the due date indicated on your credit card statement, you lose the interest-free period on your new purchases, and:

You will be charged interest on the $400 you paid off - from the transaction date (or from the posted date) until the day you made the $400 payment; and

You will be charged interest on the $100 outstanding - from the transaction date (or the posted date) until the date you pay this amount in full.

2 – False - When you make a payment, it is usually applied first to the transaction with the lowest interest rate, regardless of whether there are older transactions in the account. The result is that you are usually left with the higher interest debt (the purchases). Your credit card agreement normally indicates the "order of transactions" that is followed by your credit issuer in applying payments.

3 – False - Not all credit card issuers are the same! With most of them, you will not be charged interest on purchases you made during the month if you pay in full and on time. But with some credit cards, if you haven't repaid every penny from your previous bill, you'll be charged interest not only on the amount outstanding, but also on any new purchases made, regardless of whether you pay those purchases in full. In other words, you lose your interest-free period on new purchases because you haven't paid the previous month's bill in full.

4. – False - Cash advances do not benefit from the interest-free period (only purchases do). In other words, you must pay interest on cash advances from the day you obtain them until you pay them off in full.

5. – False - Grace periods vary from card to card. They can range from 15 days to 60 days (charge cards). Check your credit card agreement to find out what grace period you have on your credit card.

6. -- True - Visa, MasterCard, and American Express have what they call "Zero-liability policies" that protect their cardholders from unauthorized transactions. If you find an unauthorized transaction on your account, let your credit card issuer know immediately. They will investigate the matter and reimburse you in most cases provided that you file the complaint following their procedures within the amount of time that they specify (for example, within 60 days of the date of the unauthorized transaction).

7. -- False - Each month, your credit card issuer reports to the credit rating agencies in Canada whether you are paying on time. If you are late in making credit card payments, it will reflect negatively on your credit history and could seriously affect your credit rating. A tarnished credit rating could make it hard for you to get credit in the future and you might end up paying a higher interest rate on loans you do obtain.

8. -- False - If you request it be sent to you by mail, a copy of your credit report is free of charge from the two credit rating agencies in Canada (Equifax and TransUnion). You should obtain a copy of your credit report each year to ensure its accuracy (this does not affect your credit rating in any way). You may be charged a small fee for a more detailed report.

9. -- False - Since you've been carrying a balance since October, you owe interest on that amount until the day you pay it off in full. If you wait until February 13 to make a payment, you will still owe interest that accrued between the dates of January 31 (your statement date) and February 13 (your payment date). This interest charge will appear on your February statement.

10. -- False - A credit issuer regulated by the federal government must give at least 30 days notice before it can make the following changes to your credit card agreement (this list is not exhaustive):

- Increase in fees for various transactions.

- Change in your fixed interest rate.

- Decrease in the grace period.

- Increase or decrease in the minimum payment.

Credit and Debit Card Security

Using cards to pay for stuff is very convenient. Unfortunately, in the wrong hands, your cards can be used to steal your money. Do you know how to protect yourself? It is important to understand that you may be held responsible for losses if you are negligent with your cards.

The Basics:

- Keep your cards in a safe place and never leave them unattended.

- When using your chip credit card or debit card ensure that your personal identification number (PIN) is hidden and no one is looking over your shoulder to get it.

- Choose a PIN that does not contain obvious information that can be linked to you, such as your phone number or your birthday. Never disclose your PIN number, even to friends.

- Before sending your personal information (address, phone number, credit card number) over the Internet, always make sure that the website you're providing information to uses encryption to keep your data secure. There should be a padlock symbol in the bottom right corner of your web browser. As well, the end of the secure URL includes "Shtml".

- Keep track of the transactions on your debit and credit card accounts. With many accounts, you can retrieve your account information online. Call your bank or credit card company immediately if you suspect that someone else is purchasing things with your card.

- Before throwing away documents containing your personal information (e.g. credit card receipts, financial statements, old credit and debit cards, tax forms, computer storage devices, etc.), destroy them (cut up, shred, erase).

Quiz:

The following true or false questions may help you learn more about credit card fraud.

1. If your credit card is lost, stolen or used without your permission, you should report this information right away to the credit card company. True or False?

2. Credit card issuers do not permit you to lend your credit card. Lending your card may void the consumer protections you have under laws and voluntary codes. True or False?

3. If you request an additional card for a family member, you are liable for all debt that person incurs. True or False?

4. There is no need to shred an empty (i.e. not filled out) or incomplete credit card application that came in the mail if you are just throwing it in the garbage. True or False?

Answers:

1. *True*
2. *True*
3. *True*
4. *False*

Credit Decisions

In a perfect world, you would never need to borrow money. Still, most people will eventually need a loan of some kind whether it is for tuition, a car loan, mortgage, etc. Credit, if used wisely, can be used to your advantage. The key is to know your borrowing options and avoid borrowing more than you need.

The Basics:

- There are lots of reasons to borrow money, such as paying for education, buying a house or car, paying for major purchases over time, making investments or using a line of credit or credit card when your cash flow is low.

- Borrowing money can be a useful tool for building your assets. For example, education can help you to get a better paying job, while buying a house gives you a place to live and a long term valuable asset. However, borrowing to buy gadgets, such as an iPod, Wii or 3DTV, can become a major drain on your finances especially if you have to pay a high rate of interest.

- Before applying for a loan or credit card, shop around for the best interest rates and payment terms. Thorough research now could save you a lot of money later.

- Read the fine print on your loan or credit card agreement before you sign it! Knowing the terms and conditions in advance could save you a lot of money and grief later on.

- Beware of "payday" loans, which are small loans that a borrower usually is required to pay back on or before his or her next payday. These loans are one of the most expensive ways for a consumer to borrow money.

- Credit agencies keep track of your credit history - how much you have borrowed in the past and whether you have paid it back. If you have ever taken out a loan, used a credit card, signed up for utilities such as hydro, water or cable television, you will have a credit history. Your credit history is used by banks and businesses to decide whether to lend you money and how much interest to charge you.

- If you're having trouble getting credit or are suddenly billed for things you did not purchase, you can check your credit history to see if a mistake has been made.

- Know how much you owe and how much interest you are paying.

- Borrow money with care and always have a plan for paying back the money that you owe. Don't push off repaying your loan.

Managing Your Credit Cards

Wow! Just sign your name and you can buy whatever you want! Credit cards are fun, handy and… potentially your worst budget crusher. How do you choose the right card? What do you know about your responsibilities as a card holder? Do you know how much interest will accumulate if you can't pay? Keep your finances in good order by learning more about your credit cards.

The Basics:

- Because there are many types of cards out there, you can shop around to find the card that is right for you. What are the interest rates and minimum monthly payments? What will your credit limit be? Does the card offer any bonus features, like points toward "rewards", car rental insurance or affiliation with a cause that you support?

- Know your card. Understand the interest rate, any annual fees, and minimum monthly payments. Make sure you understand all of the terms and conditions before you sign the agreement.

- Keep track of what you purchase with your credit card and where. Then, check your monthly billing statements to ensure that all the charges on it are for purchases that you made. This will help you monitor your spending and avoid fraud.

- Make your minimum payments on time to avoid credit problems. If possible, pay the full balance on your credit card when you receive your bill.

- Only use your credit card if you are sure that you will be able to repay the balance soon. When used wisely, your credit card will help you build a good credit history, which will help you when you apply for a mortgage or a personal loan. When you don't make payments on time, you will hurt your future access to credit.

- If you lose your card or suspect that someone else is using it for unauthorized purchases, call your credit card company immediately. Cancel any credit cards that you are not using.

Credit History and Your Score

Your credit history is recorded by at least one of Canada's three major credit-reporting agencies. A credit report is a "snapshot" of your credit history (i.e. what you borrowed, what you have paid back, late payments, etc.). It is one of the main tools that lenders use to decide whether or not to give you credit. Your credit file is created when you first borrow money or apply for credit. On a regular basis, companies that lend money or issue credit cards to you — including banks, finance companies, credit unions, retailers — send specific factual information related to the financial transactions they have with you to credit reporting agencies.

Your credit score is a judgment about your financial health, at a specific point in time. It indicates the risk you represent for lenders, compared with other consumers.

Some credit-reporting agencies report the lenders' rating of each of your credit history items on a scale of 1 to 9. A rating of "1" means you pay your bills within 30 days of the due date. A rating of "9" means that you never pay your bills. When you apply for credit (whether it is a credit card, loan or mortgage), the loaner will have access to these scores and will use them to assess whether to provide you the credit you are requesting so it is important to keep your score as strong as possible.

Example of a credit report:

AUDREY O'DELL

Consumer Credit Profile
Source: TransUnion

March 12, 2003
This report is available until Apr 11, 2003

Personal Information

Name:	Audrey O'Dell	**Current**	123 A ST
Also Known As:	Audrey T. O'Dell	**Address:**	HAMILTON, ON L8N 3L2
		Date Updated:	07/2000
Date of Birth:	04/30/1973		
Telephone #:	(123) 456-7890	**Previous**	456 B ST
		Address:	CHARLOTTETOWN, PE C1A 2S8
Employer:	TransUnion	**Date Updated:**	01/1994
Date Updated:	09/1999		

Consumer Statement

None reported

Summary

Total Accounts:	5	**Balances:**	4430
Open Accounts:	0	**Payments:**	110
Closed Accounts:	5	**Public Records:**	0

Personal information includes your name, aliases, date of birth, phone number, employer, address, and previous addresses.

The **consumer statement** shows any comments you may have made. If, for example, you want to give your side of the story for a disputed delinquency, it appears here.

The **summary section** gives a count of open and closed accounts, delinquencies, estimated total payments and a count of how many credit grantors have looked at your credit report over the last two years.

The main part of your credit file is the **account history**.

For each financial institution that has given you credit, the current account status is shown, as well as a payment history, and summary information.

Your credit report shows how many times you've been 30 days, 60 days, and 90 days late, how much is currently past due, and your credit limit.

You can see when each account was opened, when the creditor most recently reported your status to the credit bureau and whether or not this is a joint account (with responsibility for repayment shared by someone else.)

Summary

Total Accounts:	5	Balances:	4430
Open Accounts:	0	Payments:	110
Closed Accounts:	5	Public Records:	0
Delinquent:	0	Inquiries (2 years):	3
Derogatory:	0		

Account History
At-a-glance viewing of your payment history

		OK	30	60	90	120	150	PP	RF	CO
Not Open	Unknown	Current	30 days late	60 days late	90 days late	120 days late	150+ days late	Payment plan	Reposession Foreclosure	Collection Chargeoff

Revolving Accounts: Accounts with an open-end term

ZELLERS

Account #:	1246****	Type:	Revolving account	Opened:	04/2002
Condition:	Open	Pay status:	Paid as Agreed	Reported:	06/09/2004
Balance:	$345			Responsibility:	Individual account
High Balance:		Payment:	$10 Monthly (due every month)	Past Due:	
Terms:		Limit:	$1500		
Remarks:					

Two Year Payment History:
TransUnion OK OK OK OK OK OK OK OK OK OK OK OK OK OK OK OK OK OK OK OK OK OK OK OK
jun jul aug sep oct nov dec '03 feb mar apr may jun jul aug sep oct nov dec '04 feb mar apr may

Six Year Payment History:
30 Days Late: 0   60 Days Late: 0   90 Days Late: 0

TD/GM VISA

Account #:		Type:	Revolving account	Opened:	11/2001
Condition:	Open	Pay status:	Paid as Agreed	Reported:	06/09/2004
Balance:	$1210			Responsibility:	Individual account
High Balance:	$1500	Payment:	$0 Monthly (due every month)	Past Due:	
Terms:		Limit:			
Remarks:					

Two Year Payment History:
TransUnion OK OK OK OK OK OK OK OK OK OK OK OK OK OK OK OK OK OK OK OK OK UN OK OK
jun jul aug sep oct nov dec '03 feb mar apr may jun jul aug sep oct nov dec '04 feb mar apr may

Six Year Payment History:
30 Days Late: 0   60 Days Late: 0   90 Days Late: 0

Bank Information
Bank accounts closed for derogatory reasons

None reported

Public Information

None reported

Inquiries

Creditor Name	Date of Inquiry
CDN IMPERIAL BANK OF COM	03/20/2004
CITIBANK CANADA	12/04/2003
TCRS/COTTER	03/08/2003

Creditor Contacts

Creditor Name	Phone Number
None reported	

The Inquiries section displays the creditors that have seen your credit report over the past two years.

Note: While unexpected inquiries or previous addresses can be simple errors, they can be evidence of possible identity theft. Be sure to investigate anything that appears to be incorrect on your credit profile.

Improving your credit score

If your credit score is not as high as you think it should be, make sure that the information in your credit report is correct. To get a copy, go to this website for instructions: http://www.ic.gc.ca/eic/site/oca-bc.nsf/eng/ca02197.html

If it is correct, read your report carefully to find out which factors are having a negative influence on your score, and then work to improve them.

Here are some tips, from the Financial Consumer Agency of Canada (FCAC) on how to improve your credit score:

1. Always pay your bills on time. Although the payment of your utility bills, such as phone, cable and electricity is not recorded in your credit report, some cell phone companies may report late payments to the credit-reporting agencies which could affect your score.

2. Try to pay your bills in full by the due date. If you aren't able to do this, pay at least the required minimum amount shown on your monthly credit card statement.

3. Try to pay your debts as quickly as possible.

4. Don't go over the credit limit on your credit card. Try to keep your balance well below the limit. The higher your balance, the more impact it has on your credit score.

5. Reduce the number of credit applications you make. If too many potential lenders ask about your credit in a short period of time, this may have a negative effect on your score. However, your score does not change when you ask for information about your own credit report.

6. Make sure you have a credit history. You may have a low score because you do not have a record of owing money and paying it back. You can build a credit history by using a credit card. See the next section to find out how.

Beware of companies that promise to help you re-establish your credit for a fee; their ability to change the information that appears in your credit file is no different than anyone else's! Only your creditors are able to alter this information. Therefore you do not need to pay a third party to obtain, discuss, review or make changes to your credit report.

How to Beat that Debt

Debt is one of the biggest sources of stress and depression that people experience. That is why it is critical that you learn to conquer your debt issues. Three basic ways are:

- Plan your spending according to your income

- Don't get into more debt

- Manage your existing debt

Have you lost control of your finances? How can you beat that debt? Here are ten things you can do to help your situation.

Plan your spending according to your income.

a. Keep track of spending and make a budget.

One of the smartest things you can do to get control of your finances is to start keeping track of what you spend so that you can see exactly where your money is going each month. This is the first step in creating a budget that shows your income and expenses.

Having a budget and learning to stick to it will help you free up money to reduce your debt. For more information on budgeting, see the "Budget Worksheet" later in this module.

b. Put needs before wants.

Buy what you need first. Eliminate unnecessary expenses and look for things you can live without. See the "Needs vs. Wants" section later in this module.

Don't get into more debt.

a. Keep your credit card in your wallet.

To avoid getting into more debt, use cash or your debit card instead of your credit card. That way, you'll be spending money you already have.

b. Avoid 'Buy Now, Pay Later' promotions.

When you're having problems making ends meet, the administrative fees tied to such offers and high interest rates if you don't pay on time will only add to your existing debt load.

c. **Reduce small, recurring expenses.**

Saving a little every day can go a long way. Good examples of ways you can save on costs include taking public transit instead of your car, bringing your lunch to work and reducing your coffee consumption. Eliminating that extra $2.50 coffee or $4.00 latte each workday can mean over $600 - $1,000 a year in savings.

d. **Reduce your banking fees.**

Use automated teller machines (ATMs) from your own financial institution. When you use your debit card in the ATM of another bank, you will be charged by *both* banks an extra fee of $1.50 each. Review your banking package every now and then to make sure that it is still the best one for you.

Manage your existing debt.

a. **Pay down your highest interest rate debts first.**

If you carry a balance on your credit card, then this is likely the debt with the highest interest rate. Use cash or a debit card while you pay off this debt to avoid accumulating more.

While you pay off the credit card debt, don't forget to make the minimum payments on other debts with lower interest rates. If you set aside the main part of your income towards bringing the balance down on your most expensive loan, you'll be surprised at how much you save.

b. **Contact your creditors.**

As soon as you realize that you are having trouble making ends meet, call your creditors and explain the situation. In most cases, they will work out a modified payment plan that will make it easier for you to pay off your debt.

c. **Get a consolidation loan with your financial institution.**

This means getting one single loan to pay off all your existing debts so that you have just one payment to make. For this new loan to save you money it must have a lower interest rate and a lower monthly payment than all the other loans put together. It is also important to stop using any credit cards that you consolidated into the new loan. For more information on a consolidation loan, talk to your bank or financial professional.

d. Talk to trusted financial professionals.

These may include your bank representative, your financial planner or a credit counselling agency. With their help, you will be able to evaluate your current debt situation, determine your present and future needs, make a budget and find ways to pay off the debt.

"Debt is like any other trap, easy enough to get into,
hard enough to get out of."
– Henry Wheeler Shaw

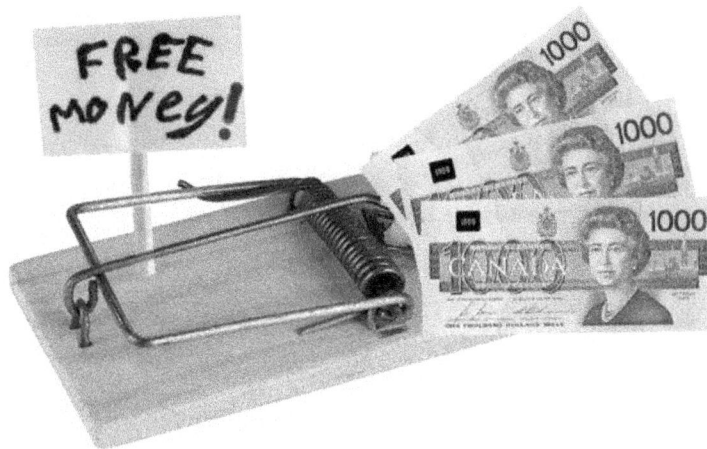

Fraud: Watch Out!

There are numerous scams and frauds out there so you really need to be alert to the bills that come in.

Credit card charges

Check your credit card statement very closely each month to verify that those charges are all yours. Sometimes people will either deliberately or accidentally charge your card for purchases that you didn't make or a charge may be doubled in error. If this is the case, contact the credit card company immediately and file a claim to get it removed.

Collection Agency Scams

If you owe debt, the company that you owe the debt to may hire a collection agency to collect the debt from you. If you do owe this money, then you need to pay it to resolve the issue before it ends up in court. However, there are times when collection agencies may call you or send you a notice about a debt that is <u>not</u> yours. If this is the case, you do not need to pay it which is why you should be very careful about being pressured into paying something that you don't owe. If this is the case, you need to respond to the notice via registered mail even if you dispute it. Review your rights on the Industry Canada site under Office of Consumer Affairs.

Other scams to be aware of:

Faked E-Commerce Websites

It begins when you receive an email that lures you to what you think is a legitimate website run by a real company (though it's not). Then you're tricked into divulging your personal information (credit card info, etc.). Banks will never email you if there is a problem with your account.

Pharming

This scam occurs when a hacker manages to redirect a website's traffic to another bogus website.

Auction Fraud

Online auction fraud involves the misrepresentation of an advertised product through an Internet auction site, the non-delivery of an item purchased through an Internet auction site (e.g. eBay) or a non-payment for goods purchased through an Internet auction site.

Job Offering Scams

Here is the setup: a company is looking for people who can receive payments from the company's "customers". They will then have to wire those funds to the company by Western Union, minus a fee they receive for every payment forwarded. The position is often described as a "Correspondence Manager", "Transfer Manager", "Financial Agent" or "Shipping Manager". This type of scam involves criminal activity (i.e. money laundering) and the job seeker is needed to break the money trail so police can't investigate the real criminal. Unfortunately, the job seeker can be charged with money laundering by police.

Social Networking sites

Scammers browse social network sites (e.g. MySpace, Facebook, etc.) for personal details that have been posted by users in order to commit identity theft.

Advance Fee loans

Ads promising "money to loan . . . regardless of credit history" lure you into paying fees that range from $25 to several hundred dollars in advance of supposedly receiving loans that are "guaranteed". Often, these ads feature "900" numbers, which result in charges on your phone bill, or toll-free out-of-province or country "800" numbers. The fee may be called "processing", "application" or "first month's payment". In most instances, you will not receive the promised loan, never hearing from the loan company again, or will be told later that you are ineligible for the credit.

Phishing

This is the attempt to steal sensitive information such as usernames, passwords and credit card details by pretending to be a trustworthy online contact. Emails or IMs claiming to be from popular social web sites, auction sites, online payment processors or IT Administrators are commonly used to lure unsuspecting victims. Phishing often tricks users to enter details at a fake website whose look and feel are almost identical to the legitimate one.

Vishing

This is a telephone version of Phishing. When the victim answers the call, an automated recording is played to alert the victim that his/her credit card has had fraudulent activity or that their bank account has had unusual activity. The message instructs the victim to call the following phone number immediately. The same phone number is often shown in the spoofed caller ID and given the same name as the financial company they are pretending to represent. When the victim calls the number, it is answered by automated instructions to enter their credit card number or bank account number on the key pad. Once the victim enters their credit card number or bank account number, the "visher" has the information necessary to make fraudulent use of the card or to access the account. The call is often used to collect additional details such as security PIN, expiration date, date of birth, etc.

SMishing

Similar to phishing, smishing uses cell phone text messages to deliver the "bait" to get you to reveal your personal information. The "hook" in the text message may be a web site URL; however it has become more common to see a phone number that connects to automated voice response system. This is an example of a smishing message in current circulation:

"Notice - this is an automated message from (a local credit union), your ATM card has been suspended. To reactivate, call urgent at 866-###-####."

In many cases, the smishing message will show that it came from "5000" instead of displaying an actual phone number. This usually indicates the SMS message was sent via email to the cell phone, and not sent from another cell phone. This information is then used to credit duplicate credit/debit/ATM cards. There are actual cases where information entered on a fraudulent web site was used to create a credit or debit card that was used halfway around the world, within 30 minutes.

False Charities

Bogus charities often use names that are very close to the names of legitimate and respected charities. The end of the year is the peak season for charity appeals. It also is the peak season for the bogus charity appeals.

Warning signs:

- High pressure or threatening telemarketers who want you to contribute immediately.

- Someone calls and thanks you for a pledge you don't remember making.
- Copycat names. Names that might be misleading or deceiving.

Dating Services

A typical Internet dating scam goes like this:

1. A person registers at an online dating service and creates a profile. The profile will include information and possibly a photograph, along with contact details.

2. A scammer contacts the person posing as someone interested in a romantic relationship.

3. The victim responds and the pair begins corresponding regularly. They may soon bypass the dating service contact system and start communicating directly, usually via email.

4. The scammer will slowly earn the trust of the victim. S/he may discuss family, jobs and other details designed to make the scammer seem like a real person who is genuinely interested in the victim. Photographs may be exchanged. However, the "person" that the victim thinks s/he is corresponding with is likely to be purely an invention of the scammer. Photographs sent by the scammer are not real. The victim's "love interest" may not even be the same gender that s/he claims to be.

5. After the scammer has established the illusion of a genuine and meaningful relationship, s/he will begin asking the victim for money. For example, the scammer may claim that he or she wants to meet in-person and ask the victim to send money for an airfare so that a meeting can take place. Or the scammer may claim that there has been a family medical emergency and request financial assistance. The scammer may use a variety of excuses to entice the victim to send funds.

6. If the victim complies and sends money, s/he will probably receive further such requests. With his or her judgement clouded by a growing love for the scammer's imaginary character, s/he may continue to send money.

7. Finally, the victim will come to realize that s/he has been duped, perhaps after waiting fruitlessly at the airport for a "lover" who, will, of course, never arrive.

8. Meanwhile, the scammer pockets the money and moves on to the next victim. In fact, the scammer may be stringing along several victims simultaneously.

In many cases, the victim will not only have lost out financially, but will also be left feeling broken-hearted. These scammers tend to prey on victims that may be especially lonely, shy or isolated and therefore more vulnerable.

Public Access Computers

Public access computers include computers shared by strangers (e.g. libraries, schools, internet cafés, etc.). Do not use these for logging into online bank accounts or any other confidential sites. It is possible that scammers have installed applications, such as Key-logger, that secretly record keyboard key strokes, therefore, easily accessing your passwords. And if you forget to log out, people can access your account.

Malware/Intrusion

This involves software designed to infiltrate or damage a computer system. Malware includes computer viruses, worms, trojan horses, spyware, dishonest adware, crimeware and other malicious and unwanted software.

Telephone lottery scams

'Winners' are congratulated on the big prize but before they can claim they must send money to pay for taxes and processing fees. Many of these scams deceptively use the name of a real lottery.

Investment related scams

An unsolicited phone call will invite you to invest in shares, fine wine, gemstones etc. These "investments" are usually very high risk, not listed on any stock exchange and will be difficult to sell if you do purchase them.

Nigerian advance fee frauds

This scam takes the form of an offer asking you to share in a huge amount of money in return for using your bank account to allow the transfer of the money out of the country. The scammers will either use the information given to empty your bank account or they will convince you that your money is needed up front for bribing officials.

Pyramid schemes

These schemes offer a financial investment based upon the number of new recruits to the scheme. Investors are misled about the likely returns as there are not enough people to support the scheme indefinitely – only the organizers make enough.

Matrix schemes

These are promoted via website offering pricey techie gadgets as free gifts in return for spending $20 or similar on a low-cost product such as a mobile telephone booster. Consumers who buy the product then join a waiting list to receive their free gift. The person at the top of the list gets their free gift only after a prescribed number – sometimes as high as 100 – of new members join up. In reality, most of those on the list never get their expensive gift.

Credit scams

Advertisements appear in local papers offering fast loans regardless of credit history. Consumers who respond are told their loans have been approved but before the money can be released they must pay a fee to cover insurance. Once the advance fee is paid, the company and the loan disappear.

Property investment schemes

Would-be property millionaires attend a free presentation before being persuaded to hand over thousands of dollars for a property course encouraging them to invest in properties. The properties involved are usually derelict or non-existent.

Work at home and business opportunity schemes

This scam works by advertising for "paid work from home" opportunities which nearly always demand up front money for materials or by requiring investment in a business with little or no chance of success.

Identity Theft

Identity theft is a crime in which an imposter obtains key pieces of your personal information, such as your banking information or your driver's license number, in order to impersonate you. The information can be used to obtain credit, merchandise, and services in your name or to provide the thief with false credentials. In addition to running up debt, an imposter might provide false identification to police, creating a criminal record or leaving outstanding arrest warrants in your name. There are two basic versions of financial identity theft

1. Victim Established Accounts Accessed

The scammer pretends to be an existing account holder in order to obtain funds from the legitimate bank account of the victim. This involves obtaining one or more identity tokens (Social Insurance card, paper cheque, deposit slip, PIN code, debit/credit card number, bank statement, identifying personal data, etc.) then using the ID token to access funds via one or more methods (branch teller, ATM, retail cashier, telephone banking, etc.).

2. Scammer Established Accounts

The scammer establishes new accounts using someone else's identity or a fake identity. Typically the intent is to use someone else's good credit history to obtain funds (credit cards or loans) or a chequing account which can be overdrafted (i.e. allowed withdraw more money than is in the account). A classic example of credit-dependent financial crime (bank fraud) occurs when a scammer obtains a loan from a financial institution by impersonating someone else. The scammer pretends to be the victim by presenting an accurate name, address, birth date, or other information that the lender requires as a way of establishing identity. Even if this information is checked against the data at a national consumer reporting agency, the bank will encounter no concerns, as all of the victim's information matches the records. The bank has no easy way to discover that the person is pretending to be the victim, especially if an original, government-issued id can't be verified (as is the case in online, mail, telephone, and fax-based transactions). The scammer keeps the money from the loan, the bank is never repaid, and the victim is wrongly blamed for defaulting on a loan s/he never authorized.

In most cases, a scammer needs to obtain personal id or documents about an individual in order to impersonate them. Some ways that they may do this by:

- Stealing mail or rummaging through garbage.
- Retrieving information from old equipment, like computers, that have been disposed of carelessly, e.g. at public dump sites, given away without proper sanitizing etc.

- Stealing payment or identification cards, either by pick pocketing or by skimming through a compromised card reader.

- Eavesdropping on public transactions to obtain personal data (shoulder surfing).

- Stealing personal information from computers and computer databases (Trojan horses, hacking and Keylogger keystroke recording software).

- Data breach that results in the public (i.e. posted on the internet) or easily-obtainable (i.e. printed on a mailing label) display of sensitive information such as a Social Insurance Number or credit card number.

- Advertising bogus job offers (either full-time or work from home based) to which the victims will reply with their full name, address, resume, telephone numbers, and banking details.

- Infiltration of organizations that store large amounts of personal information.

- Impersonating a trusted company/institution/organization in an electronic communication to promote revealing of personal information (phishing).

- Browsing social network (MySpace, Facebook, etc) sites, online for personal details that have been posted by users.

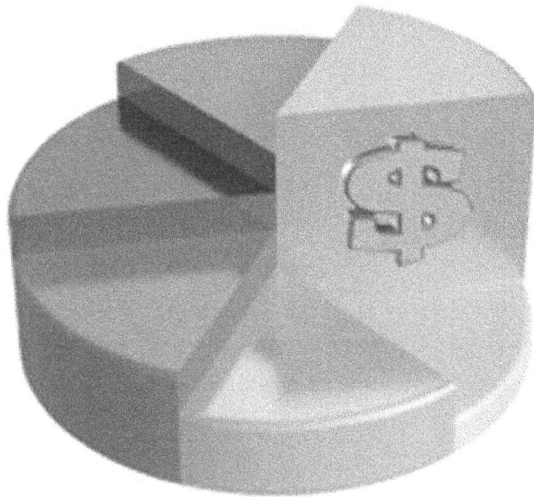

Budgets: Making a Plan

Learn to Manage Your Money

Remember when your biggest expense was candy and comic books? Well, for most of us, that has changed! As an adult, you are responsible for managing your own finances. Here are a few things you should know.

- First, do you have financial goals? Do you have a plan for how you will reach them? Can you afford to take time to get informed about financial planning, smart consumer decision-making and debt management? Can you afford not to?

- Use a notebook to list all of your income and expenses for one month to gain better understanding of your spending habits. From your morning coffee to a new home theatre system, you need to know where your money is going.

- Establish a budget and stick to it! This will help indicate if you are spending more than you should. Do you need to make some changes? Careful financial planning will help you save money for a car, a new laptop, a new video game or whatever else suits your needs!

- Watch your debt! Know how much you owe and how much the interest is costing you. Some debt may be necessary to pay for school, a car or a house. Try to avoid going into debt to pay for non-essential items such as an HDTV, video games, clothes, and so on. The interest could get expensive!

- Start saving! If you can, put away some money every month, even if it's just a few dollars. The money will start to add-up over time and be there when you need it.

- It's all about making choices: what can you do without *now* so that you can have something else *later*? In the end, you'll enjoy your life more knowing that you will still have money to save or spend after all of your bills are paid. Moderation is the key!

Making a Budget and Sticking to It

Do you shiver whenever you hear the word "budget"? Sure, a budget involves a bit of work on your part, but the payoff is financial stability and peace of mind. Once you get the hang of it, budgeting is easy and can mean a better financial future for yourself.

What is a budget?

A budget is a written document (not a mental list) that helps you take control of your personal finances. It is an excellent money management tool that can help you in any of the following situations:

- If you find that money is tight.

- If you don't know where your money is going.

- If you have problems paying off your debt.

- If you don't save regularly.

- If you want to find ways to make your dollar stretch further.

A budget helps you see more clearly how much money you receive and how much you spend and save. It helps you set spending limits and live within your means. It helps you find ways to get rid of your debt, reduce costs and have more money for things that are *really* important to you.

Before you start making a budget

Think about your goals

Before you start making a budget, take some time to think about your financial goals. Do you want to pay off your debt? Do you want to go on vacation or buy a specific item for yourself or someone else? Do you want to go to college or university? Do you want a car or your own place? Do you want to spend a year travelling?

Keep track of your money

Most people know how much money they make (income). But do you know where your money is going (expenses)? The following exercise will help you achieve just that. Every dollar you spend has an impact on the overall picture.

✍ Exercise: Tracking Your Habits

Every day, for a month or two, keep track of everything you buy, from groceries to your daily cup of coffee. Keep a copy of bills you pay during that time, and write down what you buy in a notepad or keep your receipts. Doing this will help you understand your spending habits and make a budget.

Needs vs. Wants

How often do the words "I need" come out of your mouth? "I need that coat!", "I need that iPod in green even though I already have one in blue and one in pink!", "I need that mochaccino!". But did you ever stop to think how many of those requests are actually "*needs*" and how many are simply "*wants*"?

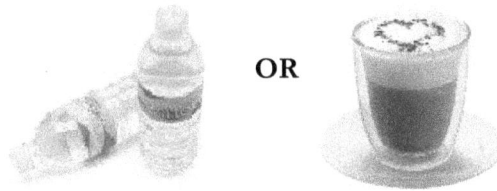

OR

To live on a budget, it helps to really understand the difference between "*needs*" and "*wants*". And you probably do understand that food is a need and a latte is a want. But some mornings, after taking care of your baby brother or working late, a latte is sure to feel like a "*need*". Maybe coffee is a "*need*" but gourmet coffee drinks are definitely a "*want*". Maybe a cell phone is a "*need*" for personal safety but custom ringtones are almost assuredly a "*want*". When creating a spending plan and trying to live with limited funds, it's helpful to really consider what is a "*need*" and what is a "*want*".

What you define as needs and wants does not have to remain etched in stone. For example, having an MP3 player could generally be defined as a want. But if you find that noise from your siblings or the neighbours is too distracting for you to study, you might need background music to block out the other sounds.

✎ Exercise: Needs vs. Wants Worksheet

Use the Needs vs. Wants Worksheet to write down some of your *"needs"* and *"wants"*. Then look carefully at what you've written down. Are the *"needs"* really *"needs"*, or can they be moved to the *"wants"* category?

Now, review your list and think about what's really important to you and what has lasting value. Be realistic (and honest)!

- Do you really need or want everything on your list? Put stars next to the items that are particularly important to you.

- Are some needs really wants? Cross off the least important wants.

- Decide if each item makes sense. If not, cross it off, or change it to something that is more reasonable.

Did this help you identify ways to save money and meet your goals?

Needs Vs. Wants Worksheet

Use this worksheet to write down some of your needs and wants and then look carefully at what you've written down.

Review your list and think about what's really important to you and why.

- Do you really need or want *everything* on your list? Put checkmarks next to the items that are particularly important to you.

- Can some needs really be wants in disguise? Cross off the least important wants.

- If you find that some of your wants are unreasonable, write down a more reasonable alternative to that particular want.

For example: is a cell phone a need or a want? Some say it is a want as you don't *need* a cell phone to survive (it is not food or shelter). However, some feel that it is a need for security and contact. So you may list it as a need but list it as a pre-paid plan instead of a monthly plan as the former is usually quite cheaper.

Needs	Cost	Wants	Cost	Alternatives to Wants

Budget Worksheet

Budgeting is one of the biggest challenges for most people. It is a great reality check if you take it seriously and are honest with your needs and wants that you listed above. For example, if money is tight then maybe you don't need all those additional features on your phone like conferencing and call waiting which can add up. Maybe you don't need the VIP package listed on your cable bill if you don't watch all those TV channels.

Making a budget involves comparing the amount of money you think you will receive (your income), spend (your expenses) and save with the amount of money that you actually receive, spend and save over a fixed period of time. Your budget is balanced when your income equals or is greater than your expenses.

As you fill out the *Budget Worksheet*, follow the steps below to create a balanced budget and find ways to reach your financial goals.

How to use the Budget Worksheet

Step	How to use the Budget Worksheet
Step 1: List your previous incomes and expenses	• Take out the recent pay stubs, bills and receipts you collected over the previous month(s). Try not to go by memory. • Separate your income and expenses in the categories listed. For each category, if you have collected data for more than one month, take the average. Add any missing categories under 'Other'. **When you are done, review the figures and ask yourself:** • Did I miss any income or expenses? • In the 'Mandatory Expenses (Needs)' and 'Other Expenses (Wants)' sections, are there any other categories missing to reflect my personal situation? • Are there categories in the 'Mandatory Expenses (Needs)' that fit better in the 'Other Expenses (Wants)', or vice-versa, to reflect my personal situation? • Was I able to save any money, or did I have to borrow (such as adding money to a credit card balance) to make ends meet?
Step 2: Create a balanced budget	Creating a budget means looking at your past expenses and creating an improved version that reflects your financial goals. A balanced budget is when income exceeds expenses—that is, you are able to save a bit of money each month. This is the ideal scenario. Your budget is what will guide your spending in future months and help you save money. • Take another copy of the worksheet and complete it using your ideal situation. Use the results from Step 1 to guide you, but adjust the

	figures as you go along, while you think of the following: • Do the figures in the first worksheet reflect my expenses in *any* given month? If not, what would be a more realistic figure? • Are there any small, recurring expenses that I can cut? • Are there expenses in the "Wants" categories that I can cut? • Do I want to add money to certain new spending categories that reflect my financial goals, such as saving for a vacation or school or creating an emergency fund? Once you are done, take total income and deduct total expenses to find out how much money you will be able to save. Adjust your expenses where you can so that your monthly savings help you meet your future goals.

Step 3:
Use your
budget each
month
	This is the most important step in the budget process. Each month, limit your spending as much as possible to what was in your second worksheet. Keep receipts, bills and lists of your income and expenses.
	
	FILL OUT ANOTHER WORKSHEET TO TRACK HOW YOU ARE DOING (Actual Spending) at the end of each month (you may want to make extra copies of the *Budget Worksheet* for this purpose) using the data you collected during the month.
	
	COMPARE WORKSHEET #2 AND WORKSHEET #3 (Difference between Actual Spending and Budget)
	
	• To help you figure out whether your spending for the month was in line with your budget, you can fill out another worksheet to track your progress.
	
	• Look at the results of worksheet #4 and ask yourself the following questions:
	
	    • Are the differences between my actual spending and my budget large or small?
	
	    • In which categories are the differences the largest? Why? Is it because of an unusual situation or is this likely to happen each month?
	
	    • Am I able to save enough money to reach my financial goals or to pay off my debt?
	
	Continue with this exercise each month. Many people make this a regular habit at the end of each month.

Budget Worksheet

INCOME ITEMS

Net Income Or Self-Employment Earnings (After Taxes)	
Income From Investments/Interest	
Government Grants/Subsidies (After Taxes)	
Allowance	
Employment Insurance/ Worker's Comp. Earnings	
Other Earnings -	
- Public Assistance	
- Canada Child Tax Benefit (CCTB)	
Total Monthly Income (A) (add all income items)	

MANDATORY EXPENSE ITEMS (NEEDS)

Rent/Mortgage	
Room & Board	
Property Taxes/Condo Fees (1/12 of annual total)	
Home Insurance	
Utilities (gas, hydro, water) (average is 25% of rent)	
Tuition	
Groceries	
Prescription Drugs	
Child Care	
Doctor	
Dentist	
Nursing Care	
Family Court Payments	
Tax Provisions	
Household repairs	
Basic Clothing	

Loan Payments	
Life, Disability, Medical Insurance	
Mandatory Savings/Emergency Fund	
Other	
Car Expenses:	
Lease/ Loan Payment	
License/Plate Registration	
Repairs/Maintenance	
Gas	
Insurance	

OTHER EXPENSE ITEMS (WANTS)

Telephone ■ Home Phone ■ Long Distance Plan ■ Cell Phone	
Non-essential Clothing	
Laundry/Dry Cleaning	
Toiletries	
Haircuts	
Meals Outside Home (restaurants, etc.)	
Lunches	
Internet	
Cable Television	
Furniture Payments ■ Can you live on milk crates? $40/month ■ Used couches are fine. $80/month ■ I deserve all new! $250/month	
Cigarettes	
Alcohol	
Recreation/Entertainment	
Children's Activities	

Gifts	
Donations	
Transportation (other than auto) TTC Metropass is $109/month	
Vacations	
Other (specify)	

Total Monthly Expenses (B) (add all expense items)	-

Total Monthly Income (A)	(from above)	-
Total Monthly Expenses (B)	(from above)	-
Excess (Deficiency): (A-B)*		-

*If the number is a negative (i.e. expenses are greater than income) then you are spending more than you are earning.

Learning to stick to your budget

Learning to stick to a budget can seem difficult at first, but the more you use your budget, the easier it becomes.

Evaluate your budget from time-to-time

If you find that your actual spending varies a lot from your budget, you will have to re-adjust the figures in your budget to make it more realistic. In this case, go back to step 2 and reduce certain expenses or restrict your spending in certain categories.

If your actual spending varies only a little from your budget, you are on the right track.

If you are not saving enough or are not able pay off your debt, find other ways to cut down on expenses and adjust your budget accordingly.

Keep up the good work!

If you can stick to your budget quite closely, you should find that your income covers your expenses and that you are saving enough for your financial goals.

Cost of Living

When budgeting, you always need to keep in mind the current cost of necessities. As prices increase far more often than they decrease, you should be aware of some of the typical expenses that you may encounter.

2010 Housing Prices

Take note of the housing prices for your region compared to other regions in the country. More importantly, take notice of the Qualifying Household Income required to gain a mortgage.

Standard Condo

Region	Price	Qualifying Household Income*
Canada	$219,000	$49,500
British Columbia	$296,000	$60,300
Alberta	$222,600	$49,200
Saskatchewan	$214,300	$49,000
Manitoba	$146,700	$36,200
Ontario	$233,000	$53,800
Québec	$180,400	$41,700
Atlantic	$163,800	$39,100
Yukon	$238,900	$55,200
Northwest Territories	$269,000	$56,200
Nunavut	N/A	N/A
Toronto	$306,300	$66,800
Montreal	$214,700	$48,600
Vancouver	$377,400	$74,700
Ottawa	$243,700	$56,600
Calgary	$263,500	$55,000
Edmonton	$200,900	$45,700

Qualifying income is the minimum annual income used by lenders to measure the ability of a borrower to make mortgage payments. Typically, no more than 32% of a borrower's gross annual income should go to "mortgage expenses" — principal, interest, property taxes and heating costs (plus maintenance fees for condos).
Source: RBC. 2010

*N/A – Not Available

Detached Townhouse

Region	Price	Qualifying Household Income*
Canada	$260,200	$58,000
British Columbia	$420,100	$84,000
Alberta	$261,600	$57,100
Saskatchewan	$252,000	$57,900
Manitoba	$166,300	$40,600
Ontario	$278,900	$63,400
Québec	$177,800	$42,400
Atlantic	$169,000	$40,800
Yukon	$230,000	$52,700
Northwest Territories	$220,000	$50,300
Nunavut	$200,000	$45,800
Toronto	$398,200	$84,700
Montreal	$230,500	$52,800
Vancouver	$486,400	$95,900
Ottawa	$271,900	$65,100
Calgary	$345,200	$70,800
Edmonton	$223,300	$51,000

Qualifying income is the minimum annual income used by lenders to measure the ability of a borrower to make mortgage payments. Typically, no more than 32% of a borrower's gross annual income should go to "mortgage expenses" — principal, interest, property taxes and heating costs (plus maintenance fees for condos).
Source: RBC. 2010

Detached Bungalow

Region	Price	Qualifying Household Income*
Canada	$324,600	$72,200
British Columbia	$562,500	$112,000
Alberta	$338,100	$74,200
Saskatchewan	$310,600	$70,800
Manitoba	$247,300	$60,500
Ontario	$335,500	$76,600
Québec	$215,500	$50,800
Atlantic	$192,600	$47,300
Yukon	$324,800	$72,200
Northwest Territories	$335,400	$73,600
Nunavut	$349,168	$81,100
Toronto	$468,000	$100,400
Montreal	$258,900	$59,700
Vancouver	$692,500	$135,300
Ottawa	$355,400	$82,500
Calgary	$419,400	$86,600
Edmonton	$311,500	$70,700

Qualifying income is the minimum annual income used by lenders to measure the ability of a borrower to make mortgage payments. Typically, no more than 32% of a borrower's gross annual income should go to "mortgage expenses" — principal, interest, property taxes and heating costs (plus maintenance fees for condos).
Source: RBC. 2010

Standard Two-Storey

Region	Price	Qualifying Household Income*
Canada	$367,800	$82,300
British Columbia	$620,600	$123,900
Alberta	$373,600	$83,000
Saskatchewan	$328,500	$76,500
Manitoba	$260,500	$63,800
Ontario	$384,400	$87,900
Québec	$255,600	$60,700
Atlantic	$221,200	$55,500
Yukon	$378,900	$84,200
Northwest Territories	$325,000	$75,700
Nunavut	N/A	N/A
Toronto	$556,800	$119,700
Montreal	$324,600	$74,200
Vancouver	$762,900	$149,200
Ottawa	$351,300	$84,600
Calgary	$432,200	$90,900
Edmonton	$367,700	$83,100

Qualifying income is the minimum annual income used by lenders to measure the ability of a borrower to make mortgage payments. Typically, no more than 32% of a borrower's gross annual income should go to "mortgage expenses" — principal, interest, property taxes and heating costs (plus maintenance fees for condos).
Source: RBC. 2010

*N/A – Not Available

Average Monthly Rent For Two-Bedroom Apartments In 2010

Region	Rent
Canada	$848
British Columbia	$983
Alberta	$1,023
Saskatchewan	$857
Manitoba	$796
Ontario	$978
Québec	$650
Newfoundland & Labrador	$640
Nova Scotia	$842
New Brunswick	$659
Prince Edward Island	$707
Yukon	$800
Northwest Territories	$1,486
Nunavut	$2,206
Toronto	$1,093
Montreal	$680
Vancouver	$1,150
Ottawa	$1,061
Calgary	$1,082
Edmonton	$994

Source: Canada Mortgage and Housing Corporation. 2010.

2009 Average Annual Expenditure Per Household

Concept	Food	Shelter	Household Operation	Transportation	Personal Taxes
Canada	$7,262	$14,095	$3,428	$9,753	$14,399
NL	$6,496	$9,534	$3,245	$9,202	$10,677
PEI	$6,720	$11,107	$3,358	$7,964	$9,564
NS	$6,682	$11,524	$3,448	$8,870	$11,090
NB	$6,691	$10,627	$3,448	$9,681	$10,720
QC	$7,215	$11,316	$2,647	$8,380	$11.985
ON	$7,284	$15,560	$3,824	$10,300	$16,133
MB	$6,520	$12,203	$3,112	$9,501	$13,484
SK	$6,344	$12,440	$3,337	$10,997	$13,481
AB	$7,778	$16,153	$4,001	$11,912	$18,830
BC	$7,570	$16,336	$3,483	$9,318	$13,157
NT	$9,509	$17,848	$4,285	$10,085	$17,668
YT	$7,496	$13.897	$3,831	$8,958	$12,905
NU	$14,815	$12,824	$4,285	$6,372	$15,781

Source: Statistics Canada. 2010.

Public Transportation

TORONTO

	Ticket	Monthly Pass
Regular	$3.00	$121.00
Senior/Student	$2.00	$99.00
Source: Toronto Transit Commission. 2011.		

MONTREAL

	Ticket	Monthly Pass
Regular	$3.00	$72.75
Senior/Student	$3.00/$2.00	$41.00
Source: STM. 2011.		

CALGARY

	Ticket	Monthly Pass
Regular	$2.75	$90.00
Student	$1.75	$54.25
Source: Calgary Transit. 2011.		

VANCOUVER

	Ticket	Monthly Pass
Regular	$2.50	$81.00
Senior/Student	$1.75	$46.50
Source: Translink. 2011. Depends on zone.		

Car Ownership

2010 Average Car Insurance Comparison

	Loan Payment/Month*	Insurance Payment/Month Ontario**	Insurance Payment/Month Alberta**
20 year old female			
New Nissan Rogue	$497	$455	$251
New Volkswagen Golf	$328	$395	$246
Used 2005 Honda Civic Hatchback	$236	$497	$276
Used 2006 Chevrolet Cobalt	$195	$470	$232
20 year old male			
New Nissan Rogue	$497	$600	$332
New Volkswagen Golf	$328	$475	$317
Used 2005 Honda Civic Hatchback	$236	$675	$389
Used 2006 Chevrolet Cobalt	$195	$540	$300

*based on zero down and 5% over five year period
**lowest basic rate as principal driver based on 3 years of driving experience.

Your Rights as a Consumer

You have rights as a consumer. Your rights come from laws governing various kinds of transactions. Knowing your rights can help you avoid problems in the first place, save you money and hassle or help you to get compensation.

The Basics:

- Always read contracts carefully and completely before signing. If you have questions or concerns, don't sign until you are satisfied with answers from the seller.

- Be cautious about ads promising guaranteed jobs, guaranteed loans, credit repair, debt consolidation or similar claims. Many of these offers are only a way to get you to send money in advance in exchange for little or no service.

- Don't be pressured into buying. If you're not sure, take some time to think about it.

- Protect your personal information by only revealing what is absolutely necessary. People who obtain very basic personal information about you can drain your bank accounts or charge things to your credit cards. They could also bombard you with unwanted solicitations and marketing.

- When shopping online, know the following before you commit to paying: Who are you dealing with? Exactly what you are buying? What you are agreeing to? How much you are paying? How the payment system is secured? And what information you are giving to the vendor and why?

- Ask about the seller's refund or exchange policy before you buy. While no legal obligation exists for businesses to accept returned items unless they are defective, it is generally accepted that offering refunds or exchanges is a critical part of developing and maintaining good customer relations.

- Always check the warranty on a product before you buy it. A warranty is a written guarantee to the purchaser of an item promising to replace or repair the article, if necessary, within a specified period.

How to Complain Effectively

When I encounter unsatisfactory services or products, I just chalk it up as a learning experience. Why should I complain?

Legitimate complaints help everybody in the marketplace. Complaints help prevent inferior products and ineffective policies in the marketplace. They also alert businesses to product quality, service and distribution problems.

How long after the incident should I issue my complaint?

The sooner, the better! There are legal time limits, depending on the situation, so act quickly.

Who should I direct my complaint to?

Always go to the seller first. All good businesses recognize a valid complaint as an opportunity rather than a bother. Be sure you are dealing with someone who has the authority to rectify the problem.

How can I complain effectively?

It is important to clearly identify the problem. You need to explain why you are dissatisfied and what you would like done to correct the problem.

Make sure you have proof of payment or proof of dealings with the business. Make copies of receipts, cancelled cheques, guarantees and any other correspondence between yourself and the business. Never give away the original copy.

The best approach is to be polite but firm. Do not lose your temper. Be persistent. Do not give up until you feel you have received a satisfactory response.

It is important that you be reasonable and fair. You should determine the business's refund policy before making any purchases and ensure that you have properly complied with the terms and warranties. You have no legal right for a refund unless the goods are defective.

What should I do if the seller refuses to recognize my complaint?

When dealing with the seller fails, you may want to take your complaint to the next level. If you are complaining about product quality, the next step is to complain to the manufacturer. If the business belongs to a professional organization or association, the association may be willing to assist you with your problem. Otherwise, you may have to consider utilizing legal action to resolve your concerns or contact one of the following organizations for assistance.

1. **Consumer Protection Branch of your provincial Ministry of Justice and Attorney General**

   These institutions administer laws governing business practices, consumer product warranties, internet transactions, auctioneers, cemeteries, charitable fund-raising businesses, collection agents, credit reporting agencies, direct sellers, car dealers, sellers of training courses, video outlets and film classifications.

2. **Better Business Bureau of you province or region.**

   The Better Business Bureau collects and reports information to help prospective buyers make informed decisions in dealing with both businesses and charitable organizations. The Better Business Bureau facilitates communication between the company and the consumer to help both sides come to a satisfactory resolution of the complaint.

3. **Industry Canada**

   Industry Canada handles complaints about misleading advertising, deceptive marketing practices, patents and copyrights, labelling, weights and measures and bankruptcy information.

   Phone: Ottawa 1-800-348-5358

   http://www.ic.gc.ca/eic/site/ic1.nsf/eng/home

   Industry Canada Web Service Centre
   Industry Canada
   C.D. Howe Building
   235 Queen Street
   Ottawa, Ontario K1A 0H5

Complaint Checklist

Before you complain, ask yourself the following questions. They will help you decide if your complaint is valid.

1. Did you gather information about the product before purchasing it to make sure that the product would serve your purpose?

2. Did you fully explain to the store staff what you wanted the product for?

3. Did you use the product only for the purpose described?

4. Did you examine the quality of the product before you purchased it?

5. Did you follow the instructions for the assembly, use and care of the product?

6. Are you unhappy with the product because it is a different size or colour than what you ordered?

7. Are you unhappy with the product because there are parts missing?

8. Are you unhappy with the product because it was delivered to you damaged or broken or it didn't last very long?

9. Are you unhappy with the product because it does not match the description or sample?

10. Are you unhappy with the product because you changed your mind about the colour, size or model you wanted?

You have a valid complaint if you answered:

- "Yes" to questions 1-5
- "Yes" to one of questions 6-9
- "No" to question 10

Back to School

> *"It isn't what the book costs.*
> *It's what it will cost you if you don't read it."*
> *- Jim Rohn*

It's no secret that going back to school either part-time or full-time could increase your future earning power. It can be one of the greatest investments that you make in yourself. However, school can be expensive. How can you finance it?

High School Equivalency

If you have not completed high school and you would like to as an adult, you can write an exam called the GED that will earn you your diploma upon passing. The GED Tests are a set of five tests in the core high school curriculum areas:

Language Arts, Reading: 65 minutes
Language Arts, Writing: 120 minutes
Mathematics: 90 minutes
Science: 80 minutes
Social Studies: 70 minutes

The examinee **must pass each subtest** with a minimum score of **four hundred and ten (410) points** and a minimum **total score** of **2250 points**. If the examinee does not pass a subtest the first time, the examinee may retest two more times, with a total of three opportunities per contract year. If the examinee passes all of the tests but does not earn the minimum 2250 points to pass the overall exam, the examinee may retest any one of the five tests in an effort to reach 2250 points.

The cost of writing the GED Tests varies in each province from $40 - $100.00. Check with your provincial GED Administrator listed below.

(Adults can also **earn their high school diploma** through the *Nova Scotia School for Adult Learning* (NSSAL).)

Passing the GED tests may require some preparation on your part. Some people prepare intensively by taking classes or studying GED preparation books and other materials. Others are comfortable with simply brushing up on a few of the subject areas where they feel they need practice. There are books that specialize in the Canadian GED preparation. As well there are prep courses. Note: GED preparation services are **not** regulated in many provinces so be careful about which you choose. Your local YMCA sometimes provides pre-tests for free to see how ready you are for the exam and also provide preparation for the actual exam. You can find a list of training options for your location on the internet.

GED Administrators

Alberta
Mr. Ross Newton
GED Administrator, Learner Assessment Branch
Alberta Education
http://www.edc.gov.ab.ca/
11160 Jasper Avenue, P.O Box 43
Edmonton, AB T5K 0L2
(780) 427-0010

Nova Scotia
Ms. Bobbie Boudreau
Manager, GED Administrator and Chief Examiner
Adult Education Division
Skills and Learning Branch
NSSAL
http://ged.ednet.ns.ca/
2021 Brunswick Street, P.O. Box 578
Halifax, NS B3J 2S9
(902) 424-0882
Fax: (902) 424-0666

British Columbia
Ms. Caroline Ponsford
Manager
Assessment Department
BC Ministry of Education
http://www.bced.gov.bc.ca/ged/
BC Mail Plus
615 Discovery Street
Victoria, BC V8T 5G4
(250) 604-2423
(250) 387-3682

Nunavut
Phoebe Hainnu
phainnu@gov.nu.ca
GED Administrator
Government of Nunavut
P.O. Box 1000, Station 900
Iqaluit, NU X0A 0H0
(867) 975-5600
Fax: (867) 975-5635

Manitoba
Ms. Marie Matheson
GED Administrator
http://www.edu.gov.mb.ca/aet/all/index.html
340-9th Street, Room 362
Brandon, MB R7A 6C2
(204) 726-6027
Fax: (204) 726-6339
GED toll-free: (800) 853-7402
Literacy toll-free: (800) 262-3930

Ontario
Mr. Ron Pelland
rpelland@tvo.org
GED Administrator & Chief
Examiner
Independent Learning Centre
http://ilc.edu.gov.on.ca/
2180 Yonge Street, 7th Floor
Toronto, ON M4F 2B9
(416) 325-4243
Fax: (416) 325-3383

New Brunswick
Ms. Linda O'Brien
GED Administrator
Department of Training and Employment
Development
500 Beaverbrook Court, P.O. Box 6000
Fredericton, NB E3B 5H1
(506) 444-3492
Fax: (506) 444-4078

Prince Edward Island
Ms. Barbara Macnutt
Manager, Literacy Initiatives
Secretariat
Department of Education
http://www.gov.pe.ca/
P.O. Box 2000
16 Fitzroy Street
Charlottetown, PE C1A 7N8
(902) 368-6286
Fax: (902) 368-6144

Newfoundland
Mr. Bob Gardiner
bobgardiner@gov.nl.ca
GED Administrator and Chief Examiner
Evaluation, Testing, and Certification
Department of Education
http://www.gov.nf.ca/edu/
P.O. Box 8700
St. John's, NF A1B 4J6
(709) 729-6261

Québec
Mr. Marc Leduc
GED Administrator
1035 De La Chevrotiere, 17th Floor
Québec, QC G1R 5A5
(418) 646-8363
Fax: (418) 528-7454

Northwest Territories
Ms. Bonnie Koslowski
GED Administrator
Department of Education, Culture and
Employment
http://siksik.learnnet.nt.ca/
Lahm Ridge Tower 2nd Floor
Franklin Avenue
Yellowknife, NT X1A 2L9
(867) 920-8939
Fax: (867) 873-0338

Saskatchewan
Mr. Ernie Lipinski
GED Administrator
Saskatchewan Learning
Programs Branch
1945 Hamilton Street, 12th Floor
Regina, SK S4P 2C8
(306) 787-8131

Yukon
Ms. Shelagh Beairsto
Dean, Developmental Studies
Yukon College
500 College Drive
P.O. Box 2799
Whitehorse, YT Y1A 5K4
(867) 668-8741

Ms. Susan Drury
sdrury@yukoncollege.yk.ca
Examiner
(867) 668-8875

For more information, go to this website:
http://www.acenet.edu/Content/NavigationMenu/ged/test/Intro_TestTaker.htm

Provincial and Territorial Student Financial Assistance

If you want to attend a postsecondary institution, but need financial help, you may qualify for financial assistance through your provincial government. Check your province's website (listed below) for details.

Jurisdiction	Contact Information
Newfoundland and Labrador	**Student Aid Division** **Department of Education** P.O. Box 8700 Coughlan College St. John's, NL A1B 4J6 Email: studentaid@gov.nl.ca Toll Free: 1-888-657-0800 Telephone: 709-729-5849 Fax: 709-729-2298 Web site: www.ed.gov.nl.ca/studentaid/
Prince Edward Island	**Student Financial Services** **Department of Innovation and Advanced Learning** P.O. Box 2000 16 Fitzroy Street Sullivan Building, 3rd Floor Charlottetown, PE C1A 7N8 Email: studentloan@edu.pe.ca Telephone: 902-368-4640 Fax: 902-368-6144 Web site: www.studentloan.pe.ca
Nova Scotia	**Student Assistance Office** P.O. Box 2290 Halifax Central Halifax, NS B3J 3C8 Toll Free: 1-800-565-8420 (within Canada) Telephone: 902-424-8420 Fax: 902-424-0540 Web site: www.studentloans.ednet.ns.ca

New Brunswick	**Student Financial Services** P.O. Box 6000 Frederick Square Room: 500, Floor: 5 Fredericton, NB E3B 5H1 Email: dpetlinfo@gnb.ca Toll Free: 1-800-667-5626 Telephone: 506-453-2577 (Fredericton area) Fax: 506-444-4333 Web site: https://www.studentaid.gnb.ca/
***Québec**	**Aide financière aux études (AFE)** **Service de l'accueil et des renseignements** 1035, rue De La Chevrotière Québec, QC G1R 5A5 Toll Free: 1-877-643-3750 (within Canada/US) Telephone: 418-643-3750 Web site: www.afe.gouv.qc.ca/en/index.asp
Ontario	**Student Support Branch** Telephone: 807-343-7260 (For Ontario students attending a post-secondary institution outside Ontario). Students attending a post-secondary institution in Ontario must contact the financial aid office at their post-secondary institution for assistance. Web site: http://osap.gov.on.ca
Manitoba	**Manitoba Student Aid** 401 - 1181 Portage Avenue Winnipeg, MB R3G 0T3 Toll Free: 1-800-204-1685 (within Canada/US) Telephone: 204-945-6321 Fax: 204-948-3421 Web site: www.manitobastudentaid.ca

Saskatchewan	**Student Financial Assistance Branch** **Advanced Education, Employment & Labour** 4635 Wascana Parkway Box 650 Regina, SK S4P 3A3 Email: SFAWEB@sasked.gov.sk.ca Toll Free: 1-800-597-8278 Telephone: 306-787-5620 (Regina area and outside Canada) Fax: 306-787-1608 Web site: http://www.aeel.gov.sk.ca/student-loans/
Alberta	**Student Funding Contact Centre** Toll Free: 1-800-222-6485 Telephone: 780-427-3722 (Edmonton) Website: www.alis.gov.ab.ca/ec/fo/studentsfinance/students-finance.html

British Columbia	**Student Aid BC**
	Ministry of Advanced Education and Labour Market Development
	Student Aid BC
	Stn Prov Govt
	Victoria, BC V8W 9H7
	
	Toll Free: 1-800-561-1818 (within Canada/US)
	Telephone:
	     250-387-6100 (Victoria area)
	     604-660-2610 (Lower Mainland)
	Fax:
	     250-356-9455
	     1-866-312-3322 (Toll-free in Canada)
	
	Web site: http://www.aved.gov.bc.ca/studentaidbc/

Yukon	Students Financial Services Advanced Education Department of Education Government of Yukon Box 2703 Whitehorse, YT Y1A 2C6 Email: sfa@gov.yk.ca Toll Free: 1-800-661-0408 local 5929 (within Yukon) Telephone: 867-667-5929 Fax: 867-667-8555 Website: www.education.gov.yk.ca/advanceded/sfa/index.html
*Northwest Territories	NWT Student Financial Assistance Program Government of the Northwest Territories P.O. Box 1320 Yellowknife, NT X1A 2L9 Toll Free: 1-800-661-0793 Telephone: 867-873-7190 Web site: www.nwtsfa.gov.nt.ca

*Nunavut	Student Assistance Office
	Toll Free:
	    1-877-860-0680 (can be used locally)
	    1-800-567-1514 (Baffin)
	    1-800-953-8516 (Kivalliq)
	    1-800-661-0845 (Kitikmeot)
	Telephone:
	    867-473-2600 (Baffin)
	    867-645-5040 (Kivalliq)
	    867-983-4031 (Kitikmeot)
	Web site: http://www.edu.gov.nu.ca/apps/authoring/dspPage.aspx?page=home

* Nunavut, the Northwest Territories and the province of Québec operate their own student assistance plans. If you are a resident of Nunavut, the Northwest Territories or Québec, contact the provincial or territorial student assistance office for further information.

Financing Your Education

Tuition fees have increased significantly over the last decade and many of today's students face financial challenges. Although most students try to keep a part-time job while studying, sometimes it's not enough to cover tuition fees, living expenses and books. Browse the tips and Web site links below for help financing your education.

Financing Options

- Scholarships and bursaries are non-repayable forms of financial assistance. Scholarships are awarded according to your academic achievement and bursaries according to both financial need and academic merit.

- The federal government, provinces and territories, individual schools and some businesses and charitable foundations also provide grants, bursaries and scholarships. Check with your school to see what is available and if you may be eligible.

- Student loans are offered at the national and provincial levels and will need to be repaid once you are finished your studies. The criteria for awarding student loans vary from province to province.

- The Canada Student Loans Program provides loans and grants to Canadians attending a University, College, Trade School, or Vocational School to help them finance their education. Check out the government website: www.hrsdc.gc.ca/learning/canada_student_loan/index.shtml

- Some banks offer student lines of credit, which allow you to borrow money as you need it, then repay the loan once you have finished your education.

- The Government of Canada offers a number of initiatives to help post-secondary students gain work experience while earning money to support themselves during their studies.

Getting Your Money

- Once you have applied for your loan you will receive a letter of assessment stating the amount you will receive, if approved. You can appeal this amount if you do not agree with it. Contact your provincial or territorial student assistance office for help on appealing your loan assessment.

- Your school will need to confirm your enrolment and you will need to sign and return your loan documents before you receive the funds.

- Tips for getting your money:
    - You may be able to have your money directly deposited into your bank account by including a void cheque with your application.

    - Meeting application deadlines will ensure that you to get your money when you need it.

Managing and Repaying Your Loan

- You will need to start repaying your loan when you:

  - have graduated;

  - have transferred to part-time studies or have dropped-out;

  - are taking more than 6 months off from school; or

  - reach your lifetime limit of financial assistance.

- The National Student Loans Service Centre assists students in managing their student loans and offers resources to help them through the repayment process. More information at: https://nslsc.canlearn.ca/eng/default.aspx

- Become informed about your loan's repayment process, including when the interest will start to accumulate.

- You will be notified by mail when your repayment process is set to begin.

- If you are unable to start repaying your loan at the designated time you may be allowed to postpone your payments. Contact your loan provider for more information.

Tips for paying off your loan faster:

- Make lump sum payments in advance, if you can. Payments made on your loan while you are still in school will be applied directly to your principal amount and will result in a smaller amount owed after graduation.

- Increase the size of your monthly payments to reduce the amount of interest accumulating on your loan.

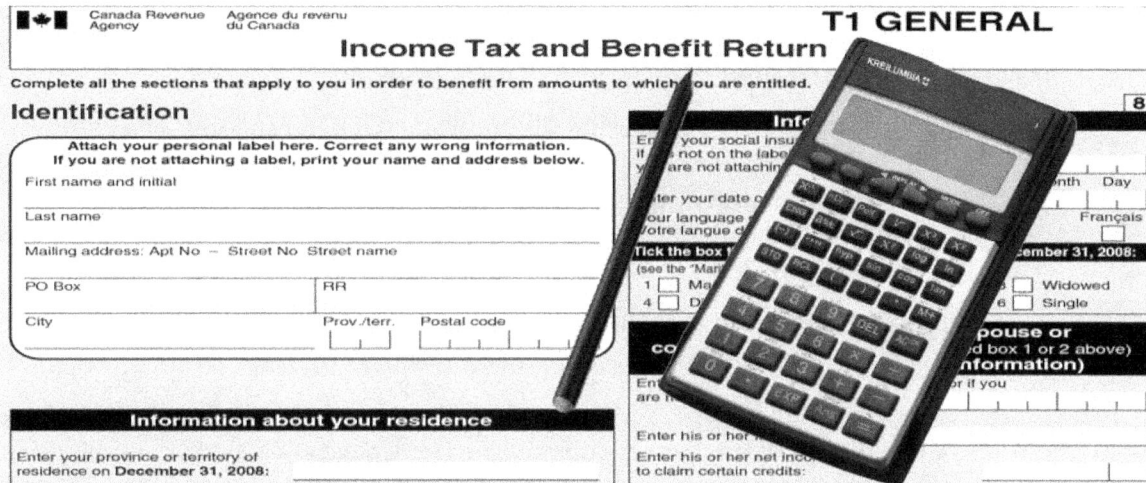

Preparing Your Tax Return

*"Today, it takes more brains and effort to make out the
income-tax form than it does to make the income."*
– Alfred E. Neuman

Have you paid your income taxes yet? A tax return is basically your report to the government of all of your income and some other financial details for a given year. While your return may show that you have to pay more tax, you may also be eligible for a tax refund if you have credits for expenses like health care, child care or school. Before you begin, take some time to learn more about taxes and filing a tax return.

- For information about taxation, contact the Canada Revenue Agency (CRA). http://www.cra-arc.gc.ca/menu-eng.html

- Income tax is collected by the CRA on behalf of the federal government, provinces and territories. Be aware of the deadline for filing your tax return, usually at the end of April. There are financial penalties for filing a late return if you owe the government money.

- Keep a record of your income from all sources. If you work for someone else, they are obligated to send you a statement listing your income and any deductions that have been made for income taxes, employment insurance, Canada Pension Plan, etc.

Use this information to fill out your tax return.

- You can fill out and send your tax return on paper or electronically. Print forms are available from several sources:

    - **On the Internet:** You can view and print the General Income Tax and Benefit Return online, or you can download the files onto your computer's hard drive. You can also use CRA's online order form to have a printed copy of the General income tax and benefit package and any other forms and publications, mailed to you.

    - **By phone:** You can get a printed copy of the General income tax and benefit package mailed to you by calling 1-800-959-2221.

    - **In-person:** You can get the General guide and forms book for your province or territory from any postal outlet or Service Canada office near you between February and early May each year.

- TELEFILE is an interactive computer program that allows eligible taxpayers to electronically file their tax return for free using a touch-tone telephone. All you need to use the service is a touch-tone telephone, your social insurance number (SIN), your personalized access code and your completed tax return.

- To file your return over the Internet via CRA's NETFILE service, you will need to purchase a CRA-approved tax filing software (e.g. QuickTax, H&R Block, UFile. For a complete list, see http://www.netfile.gc.ca/txtbsd-eng.html) or have your return filed by a professional tax service. Canada Revenue Agency will provide you with an access code to connect to their server so that you can send your data to them. The benefit of this method of reporting is that, if the government owes you a refund, you will probably receive it within 2-3 weeks.

- If you send in a paper form, include your information slips detailing your sources of income and deductions.

- Keep a copy, paper or electronic, of your return for future reference.

- After your tax return has been processed, Canada Revenue Agency will mail you a Notice of Assessment showing any changes or corrections made to the tax return (such as correcting a mathematical error). If you are entitled to a refund, CRA will issue a refund in the manner that you indicated on your tax form (i.e. direct deposit or cheque).

Do I have to file a tax return if I made under $3,500?

You do not but you may want to file one if your employer deducted income tax from your pay cheques. As you would not be required to pay tax for that amount of income, you would be entitled to a refund of the income tax deducted. If you file an income tax return reporting earned income, you will also start to accumulate RRSP deduction room limit for the future.

If you are 19 years of age or older, you would also be eligible to receive the GST/HST credit. You must apply for the GST/HST credit by filing your tax return and completing the GST/HST application area on page 1 of your tax return.

Do I have to include any cash tips as income?

Yes. It is your obligation as the recipient of the tip to declare the full amount on your tax form. However, in Québec, the recipient must declare the amount of all his/her tips to his/her employer who is obligated to report it to the government on the recipient's behalf.

The following are some examples of tips:

- A customer leaves money on the table at the end of the meal and the server keeps the whole amount;

- A customer gives a tip directly to a bellhop, door person, car attendant, hair stylist etc.;

- Tips pooled and/or shared among employees;

- When paying the bill by credit card, a customer includes an amount for a tip on the credit card and the employer returns the tip amount in cash to the employee;

- When paying the bill by debit card, a customer includes an amount for a tip and the employer returns the tip amount in cash to the employee;

Why should I file a tax return if I don't owe money?

Even if you have little to no income in the year, filing a tax return has its advantages — it's the only way to receive all the benefits that are available to you.

- If you are 19 or over, you are eligible for the annual GST/HST credit. To obtain this money, which is paid in quarterly instalments, you have to apply for it by filing a tax return and completing the GST/HST application section of your return.

- Some provinces provide tax credits for low-income taxpayers, which are paid in the form of a tax refund. As a student, you probably qualify so check out what's offered in your province. You may be able to get a tax refund even if you never paid any tax!

- If you worked last summer and tax deductions were made from your paycheque, you can probably recover most of the tax, and some of the CPP premiums, when you file your return.

- Take advantage of as many deductions as you can. The tuition fees, the education amount and the textbook tax credit may be available to you. If you prefer, they can also be carried forward via your tax return, so that you can use them in a future year when your income is higher.

- Not all of your student income is taxable. Since the 2008 tax year, all income from scholarships, fellowships, bursaries and achievement prizes are tax exempt if you are enrolled in a program that qualifies for the education amount in 2007, 2008, or 2009.

- Student loans, of course, are completely non-taxable. You can even claim a tax credit on the interest when you begin paying back the loan.

- If you relocated during the course of the year, either to get a summer job or to take up attendance at your college or university, it's possible that you can deduct your moving expenses. These expenses are deductible if your residence is at least 40 kilometres closer to your new workplace or school than your old residence was. However, they can only be deducted against either employment income at your new location or, when you are moving to go to school, against award income such as fellowships, bursaries, scholarships and research grants. Moving expenses include transportation costs such as your plane ticket. If you used your car, you can claim gas expenses and the cost of any meals and lodging en route. Also deductible is the cost of up to 15 days of temporary accommodation near your new or old residence. Receipts need not be filed with your return, but should be kept in case the Canada Revenue Agency (CRA) asks to see them later.

- Tuition fees over $100 can be claimed as a tax credit. You can claim tuition fees for post-secondary courses at a college or university or, if you are 16 and over, for courses that you take at other approved institutions to improve your occupational skills. You need an official income tax receipt to claim your tuition fees or a T2202A form but the receipt does not have to be attached to your income tax return if you electronically file. Just keep it on hand in case the CRA asks to see it.

- Eligible tuition fees include all mandatory fees charged by post-secondary institutions for educational purposes. However, these do not include fees levied by student bodies. For example, you cannot claim the following:

    o Students' association fees
    o Medical care
    o Meals and lodging
    o Transportation and parking

- On top of claiming your tuition fees, you may also claim an education amount of $400 per month for every month during the year which you were enrolled full-time in college or university. The $400 per month amount is also available to full-time post-secondary students enrolled in distance education programs or correspondence courses. If you are enrolled in a qualifying program but can only attend part-time because of a mental or physical impairment, you can still claim the $400 education amount.

- If you are enrolled part-time in college or university, you may be entitled to a special education amount of $120 per month. In order to qualify for this amount, the eligible program must last at least three consecutive weeks and involve a minimum of 12 hours of courses each month.

- The provinces also offer tuition fee and education tax credits. However, depending on what province you live in, they may not correspond exactly to the federal amounts.

- Post-secondary students will benefit from a tax credit for textbooks.

    The amount on which the credit is based will be calculated as:
    - $65 for each month the student qualifies for the full-time education amount; and
    - $20 for each month the student qualifies for the part-time education amount.

- Transit includes travel by local bus, streetcar, subway, commuter train, commuter bus and local ferry. You can claim the cost of monthly transit passes or passes of longer duration. You can also claim the cost of shorter duration transit passes if each pass allowed you unlimited travel for at least 5 consecutive days and you purchased enough of these passes to cover 20 days in any 28-day period. The cost of electronic payment cards can be claimed when they are used to make at least 32 one-way trips during a period not exceeding 31 days. Make sure you keep your passes and receipts so that you can substantiate your claim.

If you don't feel that you comfortable filing out the tax forms manually or using tax software, there are some tax preparers that will offer a discount for students. Just be sure that the preparer is reputable and will stand by you in case the Canada Revenue Agency requests an audit.

"Accept responsibility for your life. Know that it is you who will get you where you want to go, no one else."
– Les Brown

APPENDIX A: Consumer Protection Branches

Jurisdiction	Contact information
Federal	**Office of Consumer Affairs** **Industry Canada** 235 Queen Street 6th Floor West Ottawa, ON K1A 0H5 Tel: (613) 946-2576 E-mail: consumer.information@ic.gc.ca Web site: http://www.ic.gc.ca/eic/site/oca-bc.nsf/eng/Home
Alberta	**If you have a (780) area code:** **Service Alberta** **Investigation Services - North, Licensing** 3rd Floor, Commerce Place 10155 – 102 Street Edmonton, AB T5J 4L4 Fax: (780) 422-9106 If you have a (403) area code: **Service Alberta** **Investigation Services - South, Licensing** 301, 7015 MacLeod Trail S Calgary AB T2H 2K6 Fax: (403) 297-4270 Web site: http://www.servicealberta.gov.ab.ca/index.cfm?fuseaction=section:consumers/
BC	**General Mailing Address:** PO Box 9244 Victoria BC V8W 9J2 Victoria office: 5th Floor, 1019 Wharf Street, Victoria BC V8W 9J2 Consumer Protection BC Compliance & Enforcement: # 209 - 4946 Canada Way, Burnaby, BC V5G 4H7 Toll-free: (888) 564-9963 Web site: http://www.consumerprotectionbc.ca/

Manitoba	**Consumers' Bureau** 302-258 Portage Avenue Winnipeg, Manitoba, R3C 0B6 Tel: (204) 945-3800 (24-hour voice mail) Toll-free: (800) 782-0067 (24-hour voice mail) Fax: (204) 945-0728 E-mail: consumersbureau@gov.mb.ca Web site: http://www.gov.mb.ca/fs/cca/consumb/index.html
NL	**Consumer and Commercial Affairs** P.O. Box 8700 St. John's, NL A1B 4J6 Tel: (709) 729-4189 E-mail: gsinfo@gov.nl.ca Web site: http://www.gs.gov.nl.ca/consumer/
NWT/Nunavut	**Director (Treasury) and Superintendent of Insurance** **Department of Finance** **Government of the Northwest Territories** PO Box 1320 Yellowknife, NT X1A 2L9 Tel: (867) 920-3423 Fax: (867) 873-0325 Web site: http://www.fin.gov.nt.ca/
Nova Scotia	**Mailing Address:** **Mail Room, 8 South, Maritime Centre** 1505 Barrington Street Halifax, Nova Scotia B3J 3K5 Tel: (902) 424-5200 Toll-Free: (800) 670-4357 Fax: (902) 424-0720 E-mail: askus@gov.ns.ca Web site: http://www.gov.ns.ca/snsmr/consumer/

Ontario	**Consumer Protection Branch** 5775 Yonge St. Suite 1500 Toronto, ON M7A 2E5 Tel: (416) 326-8800 Toll-free: (800) 889-9768 TTY: (416) 229-6086 or (877) 666-6545 Fax: (416) 326-8665 E-mail: consumer@ontario.ca Web site: http://www.sse.gov.on.ca/mcs/en/pages/default.aspx
PEI	**Linda Peters** **Compliance Officer** *Consumer, Corporate and Insurance* **Office of the Attorney General and Public Safety** **Island Information Service** P.O. Box 2000 Charlottetown, PE Canada C1A 7N8 Tel: (902) 368-4000 or (902) 368-5653 Fax: (902) 368-5283 E-mail: island@gov.pe.ca or lmpeters@gov.pe.ca Web site: http://www.gov.pe.ca/attorneygeneral/index.php3?number =1006678&lang=E
Québec	**Québec** 400, boul. Jean-Lesage, bureau 450 Québec (Québec) G1K 8W4 Tél: (418) 643-1484 **Montréal** 5199, rue Sherbrooke Est, Aile A, bureau 3671 Montréal (Québec) H1T 3X2 Tél: (514) 253-6556 Web site: http://www.consommation.info.gouv.qc.ca/en/index.asp

Saskatchewan	**Consumer Protection Branch** Suite 500, 1919 Saskatchewan Dr. Regina, SK S4P 4H2 Tel: (306) 787-5550 or Toll-free: (888) 374-4636 Fax: (306) 787-9779 Web site: http://www.justice.gov.sk.ca/cpb
Yukon	**Mailing Address:** **Government of Yukon** **Yukon Government Administration Building** 2071 Second Avenue Box 2703 Whitehorse, Yukon Y1A 2C6 Tel: (867) 667-5811 or (867) 667-5812 Toll-free: (800) 661-0408 E-mail: information@gov.yk.ca Web site: http://www.community.gov.yk.ca/consumer/cp.html

APPENDIX B: Better Business Bureau

Jurisdiction	Contact Information
Federal	**Canadian Council of Better Business Bureaus** 44, Byward Market Square, Suite 220 Ottawa, Ontario K1N 7A2 Tel: (613) 789-5151 Fax : (613) 789-7044 E-mail : ccbbb@ccbbb.ca Web Site : http://www.ccbbb.ca/
Alberta	**BBB of Central & Northern Alberta** 514 Capital Place / 9707 110th Street Edmonton, AB T5K 2L9 Tel: (780) 482-2341 Fax : (780) 482-1150 E-mail : info@edmontonbbb.org Web Site : www.edmontonbbb.org **BBB of Southern Alberta** 7330 Fisher Street, S.E. Suite 350 Calgary, AB T2H 2H8 Telephone : (403) 531-8780 Fax : (403) 640-2514 E-mail : info@calgary.bbb.org Web Site : http://www.calgary.bbb.org
British Columbia	**BBB of Mainland British Columbia** 788 Beatty Street Suite 404 Vancouver, BC V6B 2M1 Tel: (604) 682-2711 Fax : (604) 681-1544 E-mail : contactus@mbc.bbb.org Web Site : www.mbc.bbb.org **BBB of Vancouver Island** 201-1005 Langley Street Victoria, BC V8W 1V7 Tel: (250) 386-6348 Fax : (250) 386-2367 E-mail : info@vi.bbb.org Web Site : www.vi.bbb.org

Manitoba	**BBB of Winnipeg & Manitoba** 1030 B Empress Street Winnipeg, MB R3G 3H4 Tel: (204) 989-9010 Fax: (204) 989-9016 E-mail : bbbinquiries@mts.net Web Site : http://www.manitoba.bbb.org
Newfoundland	**BBB of Newfoundland & Labrador** 360, Topsail Road, suite 301 St. John's, NL A1E 2B6 Tel : (709) 364-2222 Fax : (709) 364-2255 E-mail : info@nf.bbb.org Web Site : www.nf.bbb.org
Northwest Territories	**BBB of Central & Northern Alberta** 888 Capital Place, 9707 110th Street Edmonton AB T5K 2L9 Tel: (780)482-2341 Fax: (780)482-1150 Email: info@edmontonbbb.org WWW: http://edmonton.bbb.org
Nova Scotia/New Brunswick/ PEI	**BBB of the Maritime Provinces** 1888 Brunswick Street, Suite 601 Halifax, NS B3J 3J8 Tel : (902) 422-6581 Fax : (902) 429-6457 E-mail : bbbmp@bbbmp.ca Web Site : http://www.bbbmp.ca/

Ontario	**BBB of Eastern Ontario** The Varette Building Ottawa, ON K1P 5G4 Tel : (613) 237-4856 Fax : (613) 237-4878 E-mail : info@ottawa.bbb.org Web Site : http://www.ottawa.bbb.org **BBB of Mid-Western Ontario** 354 Charles Street, East Kitchener, ON N2G 4L5 Tel : (519) 579-3080 Fax : (519) 570-0072 E-mail : inquiry@mwco.bbb.org Web Site : http://www.mwco.bbb.org **BBB of South Central Ontario** 100 King Street, East Hamilton, ON L8N 1A8 Tel : (905) 526-1112 Fax : (905) 526-1225 E-mail : info@thebbb.ca Web Site : http://www.thebbb.ca/ **BBB of Western Ontario** 200 Queens Avenue, Suite 616 P.O. Box 2153 London, ON N6A 1J3 Tel : (519) 673-3222 Fax : (519) 673-5966 E-mail : info@london.bbb.org Web Site: http://www.london.bbb.org **BBB of Windsor & Southwestern Ontario** 880, Ouellette Ave. Suite 302 Windsor, ON N9A 1C7 Tel : (519) 258-7222 Fax : (519) 258-1198 E-mail : bbb@bbbwincom.com Web Site : http://www.bbbwindsor.com

Québec	**Québec Better Business Bureau Inc.** 1565, boul. de l'Avenir, bureau 206 Laval, QC H7S 2N5 Tél : (514) 905-3893 Fax : (455) 663-6316 E-mail : bbbbec@bbb-bec.com Web Site : http://www.bbb-bec.com/
Saskatchewan	**BBB of Saskatchewan** 2080 Broad Street, 201 Regina, SK S4P 1Y3 Tel : (306) 352-7601 Fax : (306) 565-6236 E-mail : bbbsask@accesscomm.com Web Site : http://www.sask.bbb.org
Yukon	**BBB of Mainland B.C.** 788 Beatty Street, Suite 404 Vancouver BC V6B 2M1 Tel : (604)682-2711 Fax : (604)681-1544 E-mail: contactus@mbc.bbb.org Web Site: http://mainlandbc.bbb.org **BBB of Vancouver Island** #220, 1175 Cook St. Victoria BC V8V 4A1 Tel : (250)386-6348 Fax : (250)386-2367 E-mail: info@vi.bbb.org Web Site: http://vi.bbb.org

APPENDIX C: Provincial Corporations Branches

Jurisdiction	Contact Information
Alberta	**Alberta Registries** **Corporate Registries** Box 1007 Station Main Edmonton AB T5J 3W3 Tel: (780) 422-7330 Fax: (780) 422-1091 E-mail: cr@gov.ab.ca Web Site: http://www.servicealberta.gov.ab.ca/
British Columbia	**Ministry of Finance** **BC Registry Services** P.O. Box 9431, Stn PROV GOVT Victoria BC V8W 9V3 Tel : (250) 387-7848 Fax: (250) 356-9422 Web Site: http://www.fin.gov.bc.ca/registries/
Manitoba	**Manitoba Consumer and Corporate Affairs** **Companies Office** 1010 Woodsworth Building, 10th Floor 405 Broadway Avenue Winnipeg MB R3C 3L6 Tel : (204) 945-2500 Toll Free: (888) 246-8353 Fax: (204) 945-1459 E-mail: companies@gov.mb.ca Web Site: http://www.companiesoffice.gov.mb.ca/index.html
New Brunswick	**Corporate Affairs Branch** **Service New Brunswick** 432 Queen Street Fredericton, N.B. E3B 1B6 **Mailing address:** Corporate Affairs Branch, Service New Brunswick P.O. Box 1998 Fredericton NB E3B 5G4 Tel: (506) 453-2703 Fax: (506) 453-2613 Web Site: http://www.snb.ca/e/6000/6600e.asp

Newfoundland and Labrador	**Government of Newfoundland and Labrador** **Registry of Companies** Commercial Registrations Division P.O. Box 8700, Confederation Building Ground Floor, East Block St-John's NL A1B 4J6 Tel : (709) 729-3317 Fax : (709) 729-0232 Web Site: http://www.gs.gov.nl.ca/registries/index.html
Northwest Territories	**Department of Justice, G.N.W.T.** **Registrar, Securities and Corporate Registries** 1st Floor, Stuart Hodgson Bldg. 5009 – 49th Street, Box 1320 Yellowknife NT X1A 2L9 Tel : (867) 873-7492 Fax : (867) 873-0243 Web Site: http://www.justice.gov.nt.ca/CorporateRegistry/index.shtml
Nova Scotia	**Service Nova Scotia and Municipal Relations** **Registry of Joint Stock Companies** Maritime Centre, 9th Floor, Box 1529 1505 Barrington Street Halifax NS B3J 2K4 Tel: (902) 424-7770 Fax: (902) 424-4633 Web Site: http://www.gov.ns.ca/snsmr/rjsc/
Nunavut	**Department of Justice** **Legal Registries Division** P.O. Box 1000, Station 570 1st Floor, Brown Building Iqaluit NU X0A 0H0 Tel : (867) 975-6190 Fax : (867) 975-6194 E-mail: svangenne@gov.nu.ca Web Site: http://www.justice.gov.nu.ca/i18n/english/legreg/cr_index.shtm

Ontario	**Ministry of Consumer and Business Services** **Companies and Personal Property Security Branch** 393 University Avenue, 2nd Floor Toronto ON M5G 2M2 Tel : (416) 314-8880 or Toll-free: (800) 361-3223 Fax : (416) 314-4852 Web Site: http://www.ontario.ca/en/business/index.htm
PEI	**Consumer, Corporate and Insurance Services** **Office of Attorney General** 105 Rochford Street, 4th Floor, Shaw Building P.O. Box 2000 Charlottetown PE C1A 7N8 Tel : 902-368-4550 Fax: 902-368-5283 E-mail: skfurlotte@gov.pe.ca Web Site: http://www.gov.pe.ca/oag/ccaid-info/index.php3
Québec	**Registraire des entreprises (Québec)** 787, boulevard Lebourgneuf Québec QC G2J 1C3 Tél: 418-644-4545 Fax: 418-528-5703 Web Site: http://www.registreentreprises.gouv.qc.ca/en/default.aspx **Registraire des entreprises (Montreal)** 2050, rue De Bleury, 4e étage, (Métro Place-des-Arts) Montréal QC H3A 2J5 Tél : (514) 644-4545 Toll Free: (877) 644-4545 Fax: (418) 528-5703 Web Site: http://www.registreentreprises.gouv.qc.ca/en/default.aspx
Saskatchewan	**Department of Justice** **Corporations Branch** 1871 Smith Street, 2nd Floor Regina SK S4P 3V7 Tel : (306) 787-2962 Fax: (306) 787-8999 E-mail: corporations@justice.gov.sk.ca Web Site: http://www.justice.gov.sk.ca/

Yukon	**Department of Corporate Affairs (C-6)** **Registrar of Companies** P.O. Box 2703 2130 Second Avenue Whitehorse YT Y1A 2C6 Tel: (867) 667-5442 Fax : (867) 393-6251 E-mail: corporateaffairs@gov.yk.ca Web Site: http://www.gov.yk.ca/

APPENDIX D: Answers to Exercises

Income Tax Exercise:

1) $40,000 salary in PEI

Federal:

	Up to $41,544 at 15%	Between $41,545 and $83,088 at 22%	Between $83.089 and $128,800 at 26%	Over $128,800 at 29%
Calculation	40000 * 0.15			
Amount	+ 6000	$ 0 +	$ 0 +	$ 0 =
Total Federal Tax	$6,000			

Provincial (PEI):

	Up to $31,984 at 9.8%	Between $31,985 and $63,969 at 13.8%	Over $63,969 at 16.7%
Calculation	31984 *0.098	8016 * 0.138	
Amount	$ 3134.43 +	$ 1106.20 +	$ 0 +
Total Provincial Tax	$4,240.63		

Total Income Tax in PEI: $10,240.63

2) $102,000 salary in Ontario

Federal:

	Up to $41,544 at 15%	Between $41,545 and $83,088 at 22%	Between $83.089 and $128,800 at 26%	Over $128,800 at 29%
Calculation	41544 * 0.15	(83088-41544) * 0.22	(102000-83088) * 0.26	
Amount	$ 6231.60 +	$ 9139.68 +	$ 4917.12 +	$ =
Total Federal Tax	**$ 20,288.40**			

Provincial (Ontario):

	Up to $37,774 at 5.05%	Between $37,775 and $75,550 at 9.15%	Over $75,550 at 11.16%
Calculation	37774 * 0.0505	(75550 – 37774) * 0.0915	(102000 – 75550) * 0.1116
Amount	$ 1907.59 +	$ 3456.50 +	$ 2951.82 =
Total Provincial Tax	**$ 8,315.91**		

Total Income Tax in Ontario: $ 28,604.31

Which should you use?

Buying gum and milk at the convenience store.	☑ Cash If you are buying small items then this is the best method. You can pay with a debit card but the fee will inflate the price by about 10-15%.
Taking your best friend out to dinner for his/her birthday.	☑ Credit Card If you have the cash available, then you can pay that way but usually a birthday dinner is more costly and you can take advantage of any rewards program you may have on your card.

Buying groceries for the week.	☑ Debit Card You can pay by cash if you have that much. You can pay by credit card if you don't have enough in your bank account. Debit card is best because any fee for the withdrawal would be small in comparison to the amount of the groceries. (It is a week's worth after all.)
Buying gas.	☑ Credit Card Assuming you are filling the tank, the amount can be around $40-$75 dollars. You can; however, pay with cash or debit if you have it available.
Paying the hydro bill.	☑ EFT Online banking is the way to go (assuming you complete the transaction in time) so that you have an electronic record. You can also pay by cheque via mail or directly at the bank but it is less convenient.
Making a donation to charity.	☑ Cheque Ideally, a cheque gives you a record that you made the donation. This is advantageous so that you can verify whether you receive your tax receipts for donations next Spring. You can also pay by credit card but it will be hard to remember if you received a receipt come tax return season.
Paying your rent.	☑ Cheque Never pay cash unless you get a receipt. With cheques, you can have proof that the landlord received payment when he cashes it. Landlords will rarely take credit cards or any other payment.
Getting your car washed at the annual charity car wash.	☑ Cash Because you won't be getting a tax receipt, cash is the best way for both you and the charity.

Going to McDonald's.	☑ Cash While McD's does accept debit and credit cards, the most economical is cash for this small amount of money.
Buying an iPod.	☑ Credit card Most credit cards provide automatic insurance on electronics. Plus a $200 iPod will earn you some reward points if your credit card is linked to a reward program.

Average Daily Balance Exercise

Try to figure out what the monthly charge would be based an *annual* interest rate of 28% on the following figures: (see Appendix D for the answer.)

Dates of the month	Balance
1st to 7th inclusive (7 days)	$ 500.00
8th to 14th inclusive (7 days)	$ 750.00
15th to 22nd inclusive (8 days)	$ 900.00
23rd to 31st inclusive (9 days)	$1,400.00

Answer:

First calculate the average daily balance for the month based on the table above.

Calculation:
(7 x 500) + (7 x 750) + (8 x 900) + (9 x 1400) / 31
= (3500 + 5250 + 7200 + 12600) / 31
= 28550 / 31
= 920.97 is the average daily balance

Now calculate the monthly rate:
28% / 12 = 2.33%

Now calculate the monthly charge:

920.97 x .0233 = $21.46

Glossary

Annual Percentage Rate (APR)
The yearly rate of interest that banks charge to loan money through cash advances on your credit card, charging items on your credit card, financing a car, getting a mortgage, etc.

ATM
Automated Teller Machine (also known as ABM – Automated Banking Machine) through which you can deposit, withdraw, transfer and pay bills at any time of the day.

Automatic Withdrawal Plan
A regular (monthly, bi-weekly, etc.) transfer set up to automatically withdraw money from one account and deposits it in another account. For example, set up for $200 on the first of every month to be repeatedly withdrawn from your savings account and deposited to your RRSP account without your intervention.

Average Daily Balance
Adding each day's balance and then dividing that total by the number of days in the billing cycle.

Balance Transfer
Moving unpaid debt from one credit card to another.

Benefits
Extra incentives provided by your employer including life insurance, health insurance, employer RRSP contributions, etc. These benefits are usually partially paid by the employer and the other portion is deducted from your paycheque.

Canada Pension Plan (CPP)
An amount of money deducted from your salary to pay for the government sponsored income program for the retired.

Canada Savings Bond
A government investment instrument offered once a year that can be purchased at banks and trust companies.

Cash Advance Fee
A fee charged by your bank for using their credit card to withdraw cash.

Chequing Account
A bank account that allows you to write cheques on. Usually at a lower interest rate than savings accounts.

Compound Interest
When earned interest is added to the principal so that future interest is calculated on both the principal and past interest earned.

Credit Available
Your credit limit minus your outstanding balance on your credit card.

Credit Card	A card that allows the owner to purchase items and services based on the owner's promise to pay in a timely manner. When the entire balance is not paid on time, then a sizable interest fee is charged monthly (usually between 18-28% apr).
Credit Limit	The maximum amount that you are allowed to charge to your credit card.
Credit Report	Also known as "Credit History". A record of an individual's past borrowing and repaying history, including information about late payments and bankruptcy.
Credit Score	A number that indicates a person's level of ability to repay debts.
Daily Rate	Your annual interest rate divided by 365 (number of days in a year).
Debit Card	A card that provides an alternative to cash as the funds are automatically withdrawn from your bank account when used.
Electronic Fund Transfer	Transferring money through online, email or money transfer service operators (e.g. Western Union).
Email Transfer	Transferring money from one person's account to another person's account through email. Accessible from your bank's website. There is usually a fee per transaction to send the money but not to receive it.
Employment Insurance (EI)	A specifically calculated amount of money deducted from your salary to pay for the government sponsored income program for the unemployed.
Federal Income Tax	The amount of money deducted from your salary based on your level of income that goes to the Federal government to pay for national projects such as RCMP, national defence, CBC, immigration, international relations, Employment Insurance, Canada Pension Plan, etc.
Finance Charge	Fee(s) for using a credit card including interest on unpaid balance and annual fees.
GIC	Guaranteed Investment Certificate. A low risk investment that offers a guaranteed rate of return over a fixed period of time.
Grace Period	Interest-free time a bank allows between the transaction date and the billing date.

Gross Income	Total amount of income that you made before any taxes or deductions are taken out.
Identity Theft	Fraud that involves someone pretending to be someone else in order to steal money or other items. It can involve the stealing of personal information of the victim to create credit cards or get bank loans in the victim's name. The victim is then responsible for paying back any debts incurred even if s/he knew nothing of the scheme.
Interest	A fee paid for the use of money. In the case of a savings account, the bank pays the account holder for the "use" of his/her money. In the case of a loan, the borrower pays the bank interest for the use of the bank's loan.
Investment	Financial instruments that allow you increase (and sometimes decrease) your money.
Minimum Monthly Balance	Bank accounts that will waive service fees if you keep a minimum amount of cash in your account at all times.
Minimum Wage	The lowest amount for an hourly wage allowed by law. This wage is different for each province/territory.
Mutual Fund	A collection of different financial investments packaged in one fund. As an investor, you would purchase shares in the fund as opposed to the individual stocks that make up the fund.
Net Income	The amount of your salary that you can spend after taxes and deductions are taken out by your employer on behalf of the government.
NETFILE	A method of filing your tax return electronically. You will need to use government-approved software and get an access code from the Canada Revenue Agency.
Online Banking	An internet-based method to conduct financial transactions using your account(s) to pay bills, transfer money, print statements, etc. through a bank's secure website.
Over-the-limit Fee	Fee charged to the credit card owner for exceeding the credit limit.
Pay period	Period of time of employment in which your salary is paid. For example, if you get a paycheque every two weeks, your pay period is bi-weekly.

Payday Loan	A small, short-term loan that a borrower uses to cover expenses until the next payday. The borrower writes a cheque to the lender for the amount of the loan plus fees and the lender deposits the cheque on the borrower's next payday. Also known as a cash advance.
Payroll Deductions	Amount withheld from gross salary to pay for taxes and benefits.
Periodic Rate	An interest rate described in relation to a specific amount of time (e.g. monthly rate).
Pharming	The redirection of internet traffic of a seemingly legitimate website to a bogus website.
Phishing	The fraudulent attempt to obtain personal information by using emails or SMS pretending to be from a legitimate website, payment processors or IT Administrators.
Principal	The original amount of money by which interest is calculated from.
Provincial Income Tax	The amount of money based on your level of income that is deducted from your salary that goes to your Provincial government to pay for provincial projects such as health care, infrastructure, education, justice, etc.
RESP	Registered Education Savings Plan. A savings plan for parents or grandparents to save for a child's future postsecondary education. Not tax deductible but the government will contribute some funds.
RRSP	Registered Retirement Savings Plan - A tax deductible investment account which delays some income tax to a period of retirement when one's income is expected to be lower and, therefore, at a lower tax rate.
Safe Deposit Box	A metal box in a bank rented by you to house valuables (jewellery, stock certificates, etc.) for security reasons. Only you and the bank have a key to access the box.
Savings Account	A bank account that allows you to withdraw and deposit cash and cheques. You cannot write cheques from this account. It earns a nominal interest rate.

Secured Card	A credit card that is insured with a savings account in case the credit card owner is unable to pay the credit card debt. In this case, the debt will be paid by the savings account.
Simple Interest	The interest earned on the principal investment only.
SMishing	The cell phone text message version of phishing.
Stocks	Shares in a company.
Stored Value Card	Gift card issued by retailers to be used as an alternative to a non-cash gift. Amount on card is determined by the purchaser of the card at the time of purchase.
Tax Free Savings Account (TSFA)	An account that allows you to invest up to $5,000 per year and not pay taxes on any interest earned.
Teaser Rate	A below-the-market interest rate offered to entice new credit card customers.
TELEFILE	An automated tool to file your income taxes by phone.
Variable Interest Rate	An interest rate that fluctuates with other interest rates in the market.
Vishing	The telephone version of phishing.

Index

www.ingramcontent.com/pod-product-compliance
Lightning Source LLC
Chambersburg PA
CBHW050240290326
41930CB00043B/3159